African PopRoots

African Pop Roots

The Inside Rhythms of Africa

John Collins

Contributing Editor:
Sylvia Moore

W. Foulsham & Co. Ltd.

London · New York · Toronto · Cape Town · Sydney

W. Foulsham & Company Limited
Yeovil Road, Slough, Berkshire SL1 4JH

ISBN 0-572-01150-4

Photoset in Great Britain by Quadraset Ltd.,
Midsomer Norton, Bath, Avon BA3 4BH
and printed by St Edmundsbury Press
Bury St Edmunds, Suffolk

Photographs: John Collins, Jak Kilby, Juliet
Highet, Ian Watts, Sylvia Moore, Anton Corbijn

Contents

About the Authors:

John Collins knows Africa from the inside. He was brought up there as a child and went to university in Ghana. For the last fourteen years he has been playing and recording with many of the top West African musicians and bands featured in *African Pop Roots*. John has published his research into African music in books, articles and broadcasts. He contributes to journals such as *West Africa Magazine*, *Afrique*, *Africa Journal*, *Africa Now*, *Music Express* (Lagos), *African Music* (Lagos) and *Black Echoes* (UK). In 1975 John formed his own guitar band, Bokoor — the spirit of coolness, and has released records in West Africa and Europe. He now runs *Bokoor Recording Studio* at Ofankor near Accra and is producing record albums for Cherry Red's Africagram label.

Sylvia Moore is internationally known in the world of culture and music through her writings, broadcasts, documentary films and performances. Her quest for the sources of African music led her to West Africa, where she was taught by local masters of traditional and popular music. She made many original recordings, and turned her research into a thesis, the first on African music, at the University of Oxford. Sylvia's work, especially with Black cultures, has taken her to many parts of the world. She is author of the widely acclaimed *Afro-Black Connection*, a fascinating first-hand account of an immense happening — the Second World African and Black Festival of Arts and Culture. She promotes culture and the arts through her work for international organisations, and is the liaison executive of the International Association for the Study of Popular Music.

Acknowledgements

Warm thanks and appreciation is due to the numerous musicians, researchers and friends who have provided information for this book, including: Bob Vans (comedian with Ghana's Arts Council); Frank Drake; Max Steuer and Christine Allen; Robert and Basia Andrews; Dr J.L. Harrison; Tony Amadi (African Music); Colin and Ronnie Ayers; Colin Lodge; Stuart Sutton-Jones; Jones Attuquayefio; Roderick Ebanks (Institute of Jamaica); Hilton Fyle (disc jockey); Brian Eno; Jumma Santos (Taj Mahal band); Richard Hill; members of Osibisa; Randy Weston; Paul Richards; Eddie Meadows; Peter Kunzler; Nii Nortey, Godwin Avenorgbor (Ghana Broadcasting); Fred Gales; Francis Goby; Bob Bundy; Juliet Highet; Anton Corbijn; Stan Rijven; Ian Watts; Jason Berry; Yebuah Mensah (Accra Orchestra); E.T. Mensah (Tempos); Kofi Ghanaba (Guy Warren); Joe Kelly (Tempos); Horace Djoleto (Tempos); Amoo Dodoo (Tempos); Jacob Awuletey (Tempos); M. Williams (Williams and Marbel); Professor Opoku (Insititue of African Studies, Legon); K.P. Amponsah (Koo Nimo); Robert Sprigge (History Department, Legon); Squire Addo (Jazz Kings); Kweikumah Stevens (Red Spots); Dr Wiredu (Philosophy Department, Legon); E.F. Collins (Philosophy Department, Legon); J.K. Addo (Casino Orchestra); A.A. Mensah (musicologist); Efua Sutherland (Institute of African Studies, Legon); Dr K.N. Bame (Institute of African Studies, Legon); Professor Nketia (Institute of African Studies, Legon); Martin Owusu (English Department, University of Cape Coast); F.A. Torto (Excelsior Orchestra); Victor Olaiya (Cool Cats); members of the Jaguar Jokers; Y.B. Bampoe (Opiah), K.A. Hammond; Mr Baidoo; K.M. Hammond; Bob Johnson (Axim Trio); Francis Kenya (Riches Big Sound); Bob Cole (comedian); Ajax Bukana (comedian); Mark Anthony (artist); Kwaa Mensah (concert party); E.K. Nyame (Akan Trio): James Moxon (publishing); Charles Kyle (musicologist); Ebeneezer Obey (juju musician); Johnny Opoku Acheampong; Charlie, Carol, Omar and Marimba Easmon; Cliff Eck (Bunzus); Eddie Omari Agyepong (Bunzus); Nii Ashitey (Wulomei); Faisal Helwani ('F' Promotions); Jerry James Lartey (Basa-basa); Nii Ayitey II (Basa-basa); Bob Pinado; Fela Aníkúlápo-Kuti and J.K. Braimah (Africa 70); Samuel Oju King (Echoes); Ignace de Souza (Black Santiagos); Segun Bucknor (Assembly); Joni Haastrup (Mono-mono); Victor Uwaifo (Melody Maestros); Stan Plange (Uhurus); Osei Bonsu Senior (African Beats); Roy Chicago (highlife band); Big Joe Oladele (Granadians); Angus Ukoli, Dean Okoro/Disi, Remi Akano (music reporter, Lagos); Albert Jones (Heartbeats '72); Daniel and Moses Banini (drummers); Michael Ganyhoh (master drummer); Lincoln Deku; EMI archives; David Coplan; Peter Drury, Peter Wilks, Charlie Pickup; John Chernoff; Misseli Botiano (Afrique); Kofi Ayivor; Victor Amarfio, Sammy Odoh and members of the Ghana Musicians' Union; Akie Dean; James Armstrong; Jak Kilby; Stern's African Record Centre; Ronnie Graham; Robert Urbanus; Wouter Rosingh; Brother Sam, Stagger, Aaron and members of the Harambee Two, Black self-help organisation; Dinah Reindolf (Ghana Arts Council); Willie Anku; Mike Popham Jilian Jackman; Dary Curtis; Florence Akst (BBC); Patrick and Rose Collins; Gill Garb.

Ojah playing at London Dingwalls in 1979

Introduction

African Pop Roots is the extra-ordinary and intimate story of the hidden roots of Africa's popular music. It traces real-life messages throbbing through Africa's body music — body music transported across the Atlantic to the 'new' world, where it was transposed into myriads of time-bending and mind-bending styles. Styles reflecting life styles, generated from a common heritage, all of them pointing back to African roots.

This creative explosion crossed back to Africa, exposing Africans and Blacks of the diaspora alike, to a multitude of creative sources, from which new syntheses emerged. Cross-over music from Africa and the diaspora has spread to every part of the globe; for more than a hundred years dance music has been dominated by African and Black-inspired rhythms.

What is the fascination of this pulsating life force? The world has come to know it from the outside, back to front as it were. First there were the gospel songs, the Spirituals, the Blues, Jazz — all rhythms of Africa. Thelonius Monk thought of his piano as a drum. Then there was the emergence of African rhythms through acceptable White forms such as Rock and Roll, when Bill Haley cottoned on to the popular potential of Black music — music which was driving young White Americans to tune in to illicit Black radio stations, and to pace the wrong side of town to find out how to click their fingers, move their bodies, and talk in a language unknown in their homes. Not only that, they had learned to jitterbug!

The secret was the beat. Success would mean creating a synthesis of the exciting elements of Rhythm and Blues, with Country and Western, to create something new. It was Elvis Presley who had the image to fit the music. He did not need to discover Black music through White teenage audiences, for he was brought up with it.

Then Osibisa burst onto the international music scene. Their music was born of the rhythms of Africa, intimately woven into the fabric of everyday life. They transformed the spirit by awakening and touching the senses, bringing consolation, hope, happiness and love. Their music resounded with a philosophy originating in the roots of African civilisation. When Osibisa were unleashed on the British public, they took audiences used to sitting on the floor, marvelling at superfast lead guitarists, grabbed them by the scruff of the neck and made them dance.

If Osibisa grabbed the public by the scruff of the neck, the real story has still to be told; the story of *African Pop Roots* which grabs you in the guts, because the story from the outside is only the tip of the iceberg. *African Pop Roots* lays bare the inner driving forces and influences of eighty years of popular music in Africa starting at the turn of this century. The great names, their frustrations and struggles, setbacks and successes; their love of music and of each other; their common bonds; their belief in the power of body rhythm to penetrate the zones surrounding each individual with life force and burning energy, and to take care of physical and emotional needs.

Here are the personal stories of the artists, as they have never

8

been told before — based on their life experiences and the living memories of the older generation; their tales of long ago. We get behind the screen of the glossy paraphernalia of the superstars, and hear personal anecdotes about the way they live, their families and friends, life on the road and on palm-wine days.

Cross-overs are charted from the roots. Everyone knows of the flourishing of styles inspired by the Spirituals: Blues, Jazz, the Latin beat, Salsa, Soul, Funk, Reggae and Disco; styles shaped in South America, the Caribbean and the USA. But what about Minstrelsy, popular already in the early 1900s in West Africa, along with the movies of Al Jolson.

Who knows about the Vaudeville and Ragtime hits in West Africa in the 1920s? Then Swing was the rage — brought in by the Allied troops stationed there during the Second World War. It was soon taken up by local dance bands.

Jazz went to Africa in the fifties. For Randy Weston, it was the realisation that 'we in The United States are just simply an extension of Africa, being like almost the beginning of life itself, and it's thrown itself out in different parts of the world. I heard music that sounded like everything from Louis Armstrong to Bessie Smith'.

Satchmo visited West Africa in 1956 and 1962. The All Stars and Satchmo were welcomed at Accra airport by a massed band of top Ghanaian dance band musicians.

Soul met soul with James Brown; and there was Cha Cha Cha, Bolero, Samba and Rumba. From Ragtime to Reggae, from Spiritual to funky Disco, *African Pop Roots* shows the impact of these cross-overs on the exploration of creative energy, generated from an ancient vision of cosmic life, moving the world of nature and spirit through body rhythms. Africa reaped the harvest of its own seeds.

The traditions after all were in full vibration: a rich musical heritage for feeling and for expressing all aspects of life from womb and tomb and beyond. The explosion came from the inside, from these traditions. There were the folk theatres such as the Yoruba Apidan travelling theatre and Okumkpa, both in Nigeria. Herbert Ogunde and Baba Mero developed Yoruba theatre from these forms.

The synthesis of Minstrelsy and folk theatre produced 'Bob', a contemporary clown, similar to the traditional spider hero, Ananse, well known in Ghana for his tricks as a major character in folk tales and traditional drama. Then there were the play dances; unscripted plays were taken around the country by concert groups such as the Jaguar Jokers. These musicals would go on for hours, so that actors could take a nap and wake up at the right cue to do their piece.

Concert Parties were the stamping ground for the Highlife boom. The pounding fusion of religious belief, Pop and traditional music led to Juju music. Benin Ozzidi music for example, dedicated to an Ijaw god. Sunny Ade, leader of Nigeria's African Beats, thinks of Juju music as his shrine — as does Fela Aníkúlápo-Kuti of his Afrobeat.

African Pop Roots explores other fusions, such as South

African Kwela, Congo Jazz, Sierra Leone Meringa, Afro-rock, Afro-disco. The great names are there — Miriam Makeba, Manu Dibango with Soul Makossa, Franco, E.T. Mensah, Victor Uwaifo, Ebeneezer Obey — to mention a few.

African Pop Roots not only presents the outstanding personalities, the developments in cross-overs, and a whole way of life. It is also a cameo of historical episodes on the life of a continent: the colonial intrusions of forts, ports and military; insights into what it was like to live in Monrovia, Liberia, in the nineteenth century, when the American Liberians settled there, bringing along the quadrille and their own cultural resources, developed in exile.

Finally, the book exposes the global reach of the roots of Pop — inside rhythms. The Ethiopian, Rastafarian and Afro-Muslim groups; and the search of Western super stars, all returning to Africa. There was Ginger Baker of Cream, and Paul McCartney with Wings, who went to Nigeria, followed by Mick Fleetwood of Fleetwood Mac

in 1980. White Jazz musicians turn more and more to the African roots. Roots shaped by a dynamic philosophy of cool and hot, cool being the metaphysical centre of body rhythms, of the laid back energy of Highlife, of the spaciness of Afro-beat, of the happy energy of Afro-rock.

The full circle has turned. As Guy Warren, Ghana's famous drummer said, 'Our artists leave home in search of a new sound, and they end up by going back home.' Equalisation is about to occur, and this book delves into the past and present of popular African music with its outstanding sounds and personalities, starting with the current music happenings, and then taking you back to the vortex of it all, the ancient vibrations and wisdom of Africa.

Section One is about the sounds and personalities of today.

Section Two deals with a process operating within modern African music — African and Black musical feedback. There has been continuous self-fertilisation of Black music — coming from the Americas and the Caribbean back to Africa,

where it has blown the lid off the colonial strait-jacket in the field of arts.

Section Three describes the movement in the opposite direction, the flow of modern African dance music outwards, to the rest of the world, affecting Jazz, Rock, Salsa, and even New Wave.

Section Four, Roots, explores the history of the birth and evolution of contemporary African styles of dance music, tracing their continuity with the traditional music and wisdom of Africa.

Section Five deals with music business in Africa, the growth of the African record industry and the music unions.

Major themes and personalities have been selected from the vast, rich arena of African popular music. John's research for the book's main themes is drawn from exclusive first-hand encounters. Sylvia, as co-researcher, integrated and edited the manuscript and added her own first-hand original photos and sources.

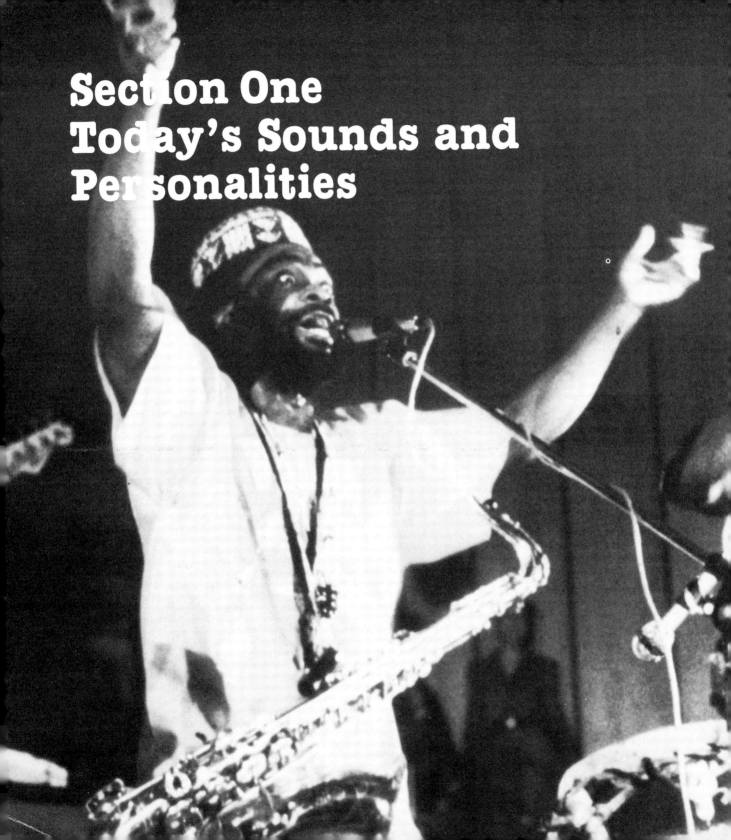

Section One
Today's Sounds and
Personalities

1 Fela and the Afro-beat Revolution

The most spectacular musical figure to come out of Africa in the seventies is Fela Aníkúlápo-Kuti, creator of Afro-beat — a fusion of Jazz, Soul and West African Highlife music. His new beat is pounding out everywhere in Africa, and is even catching on in the West. His blunt anti-establishment lyrics have made him the Bob Dylan and Mick Jagger of Africa.

Everywhere he goes, people stop what they are doing, shout his name, and give him the Black Power salute. Once, at the Surulere football stadium in Lagos, he received an overwhelming ovation, greater even than the Head of State had received. Fela had a larger retinue, with scores of musicians, chorus girls, dancers, bodyguards and wives accompanying him.

In 1974, at the same stadium, there was another demonstration of his popularity during a Jimmy Cliff show. Towards the end of the reggae star's performance, Fela was spotted by the crowd and a huge roar went up. The crowd carried Fela on their shoulders down to the stage in the middle of the football pitch, and moved around the field. Jimmy Cliff decided that there was no point in going on with the show after that.

The 'Kalakuta Republic'

Before it was burnt down by the army, Fela's home-base was in the ghetto area of Lagos known as Mushin, just across the road from his club, the Africa Shrine. He called his house the 'Kalakuta

Fela and members of the Africa 70

13

Republic', which in Swahili means 'Rascal's Republic'. A name, he explained, that he got from the wall of a Lagos prison cell. 'It was when I was in a police cell at the CID headquarters in Lagos, called Alagbon Close. The prisoners called the cell I was in "The Kalakuta Republic". So if rascality is going to get us what we want we will use that name, because we are dealing with corrupt people so we have to deal rascally with them.'

In every way the 'Kalakuta' was a republic. It has its own rules, court, prison, clinic, and barbed-wire security system. Fela lived inside with his musicians, dancers, twenty-seven wives, his brother, mother and three children, Femi, Sola and Yeni; not to mention a donkey, a baboon and an Alsatian dog. Fela ruled the place like a traditional chief. Attendants waited on him, he fined and punished wrong-doers and held court every day for visitors.

From his 'Kalakuta Republic' he, and his entourage, used to travel the short distance to his Africa Shrine on donkeys. All traffic would stop on the Agege Motor Road until he and his people had passed.

Fela at the Africa Shrine

The shows at the Africa Shrine always start with Fela as Chief Priest, pouring a libation, at a small shrine, to Kwame Nkrumah and other leaders of Pan Africanism. A shrouded figure of death then leaps on stage, and the show begins with the Africa 70 band warming up. Fela then comes on stage and has his sax clipped on by an attendant.

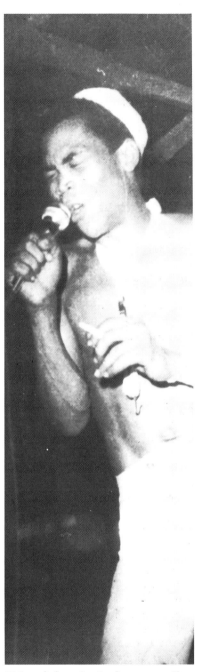

Fela, injured during a police attack on his home, is back on stage the following day

While playing, Fela is always flanked by two musicians playing clips and maraccas. The rest of the band is stretched out behind him and includes trumpeters, sax players, guitarists, conga drummers and a trap-drummer, originally Tony Allen. Half a dozen chorus girls perform. His Afro-sexy dancers gyrate on the dance floor, standing on raised platforms. Fela has a foot switch attached to these platforms. If one of the dancers tires, or is not up to standard, Fela switches off her platform light and a fresh dancer takes her place.

Expensive shit and other songs

The music of Fela and his Africa 70 is famous throughout Nigeria and Africa.

A very popular number called *Shakara* is about the way Nigerian women demean themselves by copying Europeans. Here are some verses from it:

Shakara
I want to tell you about lady-o
She go say she equal to man,
She go say she got power like
    man,
She go say anything man do
    she self fit (can) do.
(But) African women go
    dance, she go dance the fire
    dance.
She know man na (is) master,
She go cook for him,
She go do anything he say,
But lady no be so,
Lady na (is) master.

Another song which condemns Westernised Nigerian women is

14

Yellow Fever about the use of bleaching creams. A song on the same theme about men is *Gentleman*. Fela would rather be a natural or 'original' African man, rather than dress up in a European suit. *Confusion* is another of his songs about the problems of modern life.

Confusion

Them be three men wey (who)
    sell for road-side-o,
Them three speak different
    languages-o,
Them speak Lagos, Accra and
    Conakry,
One man comes pay them
    money-o,
He pay them for pound, dollars
    and French money,
He remain for them to share-o,
Me, I say no confusion be
    that-o?
(i.e. it will take them hours to
    work out the change)

A very political song of his is *No Bread*.

No Bread

For Africa here, him to be home,
Land boku (plenty) from north
    to south,
Food boku from top to down,
Gold de underground like water,
Diamond de underground like
    sand,
Oil de flow underground like
    river,
(but) everything go for overseas
Na from here it de come?

In between songs Fela speaks to his audience about Black consciousness, the colonial heritage, government corruption and mismanagement and, of course, the need to legalise NNG, or Natural Nigerian Grass, for he hates anyone to call it Indian hemp.

He has been charged several times with possession of this leaf and once the police thought he swallowed the evidence. They examined his stools, but could find no trace of the weed. Fela made the incident into a song called *Expensive Shit*. On the front of the record cover was written, 'The men in uniform alleged I swallowed a quantity of Indian hemp. My shit was sent for lab test, result negative, which brings us to *Expensive Shit*.'

Trouble at the 'Kalakuta'

Fela is always turning his problems and palavers into music. For instance, inside the 'Kalakuta', one of his girls had been misbehaving and was put inside a little prison in the backyard called the Kala Kosu. It was a symbolic prison, though, as the door was only tied with string. But she kept up such a racket that she was let out into a circle of Kalakuta people. She shouted at them and they shouted back, calling and replying, so they soon had a song going.

A more serious incident is described in Fela's song *Kalakuta Show*, about an attack on his house in 1974 by sixty riot police. They were looking for a young girl who had been playing truant from home, and who was believed to have become one of Fela's dancers.

By coincidence I was at the Shrine (Empire Hotel) at the time, staying with a group of Ghanaian musicians on a recording trip. None of us had been in Lagos before and our manager warned us about the place the first night we arrived. Sure enough the very next morning we woke up retching to tear gas, as we were across the road and down-wind of the 'Kalakuta'. We could see the whole thing including the stiff resistance put up by Fela's people, who were throwing stones, and anything they could get their hands on, from the roof of the 'Kalakuta' down onto the police.

There was a show that night, so Fela's stand-in, his lawyer, known as 'Feelings' took over the singing. By the next day an injured Fela was back on stage joking about the bandages on his head that made him look like the Pope.

The day after that he had more trouble, a court case involving Indian hemp, but he won the case and a crowd of thousands followed him back from the court to Mushin, creating yet another 'go slow' (traffic jam) in overcrowded Lagos.

Because of his continual dicing with danger, Fela changed his name from Ransome-Kuti to Aníkúlápo-Kuti, which means a person who carries death in his pocket. One only has to travel with Fela to know what this means. He loves driving and racing Mercedes Benz cars. He lets them begin to overtake and then steps on the gas. It's neck and neck at speed. Fela would never give way, even with a truck coming the other way. In this test of wills, Fela always comes out on top and the other driver has to give way. This puts all of Fela's people into a good humour.

Fela's most serious confrontation with the establishment was just after the Black Arts Festival, FESTAC (the Second World

African and Black Festival of Arts and Culture, held at Lagos and Kaduna). Fela had been needling the authorities for some time before this. He and his cultural organisation, the Young African Pioneers (YAP), had distributed half a million pamphlets criticising the recently introduced law of on-the-spot whippings for motor offences. They thought it would not be a good idea for the black visitors to FESTAC to see these whippings. Then he and his YAP released another half a million pamphlets condemning the organisers of FESTAC itself. On top of this he released an album called *Zombie* blasting the military mentality of the establishment.

In fact because of this record the term 'zombie' has become a term of abuse for the military throughout Africa.

The final straw for the establishment came when a couple of Fela's people set fire to a motorbike belonging to a soldier from a nearby barracks. The soldiers hit back by raiding the 'Kalakuta', beating up everyone there, and setting fire to the premises, completely gutting it. Fela moved to a new 'Kalakuta' which is heavily fortified. A later release, *Coffin for Head of State*, refers to this incident. The fold-open cover is a montage of newspaper clippings about the army's burning of Fela's original Kalakuta home.

Getting started

What is the story behind this famous musician, who is such a stimulus to the music industry, and such a thorn in the side of the establishment? To start with, his parents were famous. His father was a leading Yoruba educationalist and a Reverend Minister. His mother, Fulilayo Ransome-Kuti, was a leading political figure in Nigeria until her death. Even Fela's grandfather was well known as a musician. He wrote Christian Yoruba hymns for the piano, some of which were recorded by EMI in the 1920s. Fela talked about his grandfather:

> He was a preacher and was responsible for bringing Christianity to the Yoruba country here, which I think is very bad, so I have to undo what he has done. His mistakes are colonial and we are now trying to get the colonial thing out.

Fela was brought up in Abeokuta and began his musical career as a highlife musician with the Cool Cats dance band of Victor Olaiya, based in Lagos. He formed his own highlife group in England called the Highlife Rakers, when he was studying music at Trinity College, London. While in England he was influenced by the jazz music of Miles Davis, John Coltrane and Thad Jones.

When he returned to Nigeria in 1963 he formed his Koola Lobitos, which combined Highlife and Jazz, with Fela on trumpet. During the sixties his band was based at the Afro-spot (Kakadu Club) in Yaba and competed with other Highlife bands of the time like Rex Lawson's, Roy Chicago's and Eddie Okonta's. The Koola Lobitos got a big boost when they backed Millicent Small and Chubby Checker in their tours of Nigeria in the mid-sixties. (Millie,

One of Fela's many wives

16

from Jamaica, of *My Boy Lollipop* fame, and Chubby Checker, the Black Twist king from the States.) But generally Fela's music did not catch on in a big way, so he went to the USA in 1969. There, in Los Angeles, he came into contact with Black militants. And, as he explains, what he discovered there completely revolutionised his approach to music.

6 You see at the beginning, my musical appreciation was very limited, but later I got opened to many Black artists. And I saw that in Africa we were not open, as at that time they only let us hear what they wanted us to hear. When you played the radio, it was controlled by the government and the White man played us what he wants. So we didn't know anything about Black music. In England I was exposed to all these things, but in Africa they cut us off. It was after I was exposed that I started using Jazz as a stepping-stone to African music. Later, when I got to America, I was exposed to African history which I was not even exposed to here. It was then that I really began to see that I had not played African music. I had been using Jazz to play African music, when really I should be using African music to play Jazz. So it was America that brought me back to myself. 9

When he came back from the USA, Fela changed the name of his band to the Africa 70 and concentrated solely on his Afro-beat. His first two Afro-beat singles, *Jeun Koku* (Chop and quench) and *Who Are You*, were instant hits in Africa. Then the band went to

John Collins as a colonial education officer and Fela in short trousers as a schoolboy, during the filming of The Black President

London and recorded their first album at the famous Abbey Road studio. Since then, the Africa 70 has released a string of successful albums for EMI and Decca West Africa.

During this time, the Africa Shrine became a focus for musicians from Africa and abroad. Ginger Baker, the drummer with Cream, came down and did a live recording with Fela; so did Sandra Daniels, an Afro-American vocalist he met in Los Angeles, who recorded *Upside Down* with the Africa 70. Paul McCartney and Wings also hung around the Shrine for a time.

The Black President

By 1977 Fela thought it time to make a film of his life. He teamed up with the Ghanaian producer Faisal Helwani, the Ghanaian poet and film director Alex Oduro, and the Ghana film crew. The film was called *The Black President* and was shot in Accra, Lagos and Abeokuta. (I played the part of a colonial education officer called Inspector Reynolds.)

Unfortunately, after the filming and recording was completed, the soundtrack was destroyed during the army attack on the 'Kalakuta Republic' in 1977. But re-dubbing is now taking place.

Since that attack Fela has moved both his 'Kalakuta Republic' and his Africa Shrine and is still pumping out his music, now with his son, Femi, up on stage, playing sax. The Africa 70 have made several international tours, particularly to Italy and Germany, and their music is definitely catching on in the West. These European tours were great successes, and they played to audiences of around ten thousand in Brussels, Vienna and Strasbourg — and a packed fifteen thousand at the famous Hippodrome in Paris.

The last time I saw Fela play was at the Amsterdam Woods in the summer of 1981, on one of his European tours. On that trip he brought with him several hundred copies of his latest album *ITT* (International Thief Thief), the lyrics of which condemn the machinations of the American multi-national company of that name. At the press conference after the show the questions were all about Fela's attitude to women (he had all twenty-seven of his wives with him on the tour) and many of the reporters could not understand how he could claim to be a progressive on the one hand and yet dominate a large harem of wives on the other. One Dutch woman accused him of having no respect for women but Fela replied that women had their own specific duties to perform and that he would never enter a woman's kitchen as it is her domain. He went on to say that in Africa categories like male and female, old and new, day and night are never mixed up as, 'Nature is clear with no confusions'. He added that unisex and uniformity may be fine for Europe but would never work in Africa. Indeed Fela actually uses sexual polarity and tension to create energy for his music — as in the case described earlier where one of his dancers broke the Kalakuta house rules.

I visited Fela, J.K. Braimah and the band, now called the Egypt 80, at their hotel and met a very vexed Fela. He had just discovered that his British tour had been cancelled due to visa problems and put it down to the world of the American CIA and ITT. He talked about the psychological warfare these organisations used against 'Third World', countries in terms of language. He could not see why the terms 'third', 'undeveloped', or even worse 'non-aligned' should be used. Non-aligned, for instance, means not straight, crooked or bent — all which imply inferiority.

His annoyance with all these derogatory terms found expression in an album the Africa 70 released in 1982, called *Original Sufferhead* (Arista label SPART 1171). Here are a few lines from the title track:

Those who dey for London live like lords,
Those who dey for New York live like Kings,
We wey ele (live) for Africa live like servants,
United Nations dem come get name for us, dem call us undeveloped nations,
We must be undeveloped to stay ten-ten in one room,
Dem dey call us third world,
We must be craze for head to sleep in dustbin,
Dem dey call us non-aligned nations.
We must be craze for head to sleep under bridge-o.

Anyone interested in more information on Fela should obtain Carlos Moore's book on this controversial musician, *A bitch of a life* published by Allison and Busby.

2 The Juju Boom

If it's slow, spacey music you like, then modern Nigerian Juju music is for you. Juju is a more relaxed type of guitar band dance music than Highlife. It comes from western Nigeria where it grew out of a fusion of local Yoruba music and of Highlife, like Gombe, Konkomba and Ashiko — a fusion which emerged way back in the thirties and forties with Juju pioneers like mandolin player Tunde King, banjoist Ojoge Daniels and guitarist Ayinde Bakare.

In the fifties the most popular exponents of Yoruba guitar band music were the Blue Spots whose leader, I.K. Dairo, electrified Juju music and recorded literally hundreds of records. He was awarded the MBE for his successes in the music field.

However, in spite of Dairo's success, up to the mid-sixties Juju music was a poor relation to Highlife, as it was street music played in palm-wine bars, at weddings and traditional functions. The top-notch night-clubs were in the grip of Highlife fever, and most recordings were made of Highlife.

Everything changed with the Nigerian Civil War, including the sound and popularity of Juju music. First of all, many of the top Highlife bands in Lagos had been run by easterners and therefore broke up. Only a few dance bands were left in the Lagos area, like Bobby Benson's, Victor Olaiya's and Roy Chicago's. Even Roy Chicago's band collapsed when his musicians were drafted into the army as musicians. From this point on, Juju music had the field to itself, in Lagos and western Nigeria. Whereas Highlife continues to be popular in the east of the country, it has never recovered popularity in the west — there it's Juju all the way.

Since then, and right up to the present, the Juju field has been dominated by two outstanding musicians who brought about the main changes in Juju music — Ebeneezer Obey who slowed down the music of I.K. Dairo to a rock-steady beat; and the younger Sunny Ade, who retained the slow tempo but added some ultra-modern effects and a steel guitar.

Ebeneezer Obey

I visited Ebeneezer at his home off Palm Avenue in the Mushin area of Lagos, and he told me that the first bands he ever joined, in the fifties, were the Royal Mambo Orchestra and the Guinea Mambo Orchestra. He moved on to Fatal Rolling Dollars Band and the Federal Rhythm Brothers, before forming his own band in 1964, the International Brothers, formed after he had been offered a recording contract by Decca West Africa (Afrodisia). Their first release was the single *Ewa Wowun Ojumi Ri* (People Come and See What I See), after which they released a series of albums for Decca.

In 1970 he changed the name of the band to Chief Commander Ebeneezer Obey and the Inter-reformers Band and continued to release on the Afrodisia label. One very popular song was dedicated to the *Late General Murtala*

Sunny Ade

Ebeneezer Obey

Muhammed and another expounded the government policy of *Operation Feed the Nation*. Many of his songs have a strong moral behind them, like one about a man, his son and their donkey. When the father rode the donkey, people called him selfish. When they both rode it they were accused of being cruel to animals. When neither rode but walked behind, they were thought mad. Obey's songs are so popular that on a new album his advance orders alone are over one hundred thousand copies.

The Inter-reformers today are an eighteen-piece band based at Obey's night-club in Lagos, the Miliki Spot. The group's instruments include electric guitars, wooden tambourines, the squeeze or talking drum, the shekeres (maraccas), agogo (clips) and Goumbeh or Gombe drums. His own pair of Goumbeh drums are traditional hand-carved drums which have a modern drum-head with screws, rather than wooden drum-pegs.

Compared to the earlier type of fifties Juju music, which I.K. Dairo used to play, Ebeneezer Obey's style is much slower and more spacey. In fact the Juju music of the fifties was more similar in tempo to the fast and bubbly Highlife music of West Africa, than to the ultra-relaxed Juju music of today. It is so relaxed, and the live shows are so long, that the bandsmen often sit down behind their amplifiers when playing in public. Not only do the musicians weave a web of cool rhythms together, but they also embroider and cross the main melody with snatches of other tunes.

Ebeneezer Obey's band is typical of many of the hundreds of Juju bands. In all of them the bass guitar is used like a bass drum; traditional percussion is used a lot and horns are never used. Like many other bands much of the music of the Inter-reformers is praise music, praising God as in Yoruba hymns (Adura), or praising big men and patrons. Sometimes huge sums of money are showered over Ebeneezer and his bandsmen by flattered patrons, who will try to stick hundreds of naira on the musicians' moist brows.

Sunny Ade

Equally popular is Obey's young rival, Sunny Ade, who has brought Juju music right up to date. His band, the African Beats, not only uses the guitars and traditional percussion of orthodox Juju, but also the vibraphone, moog synthesiser and steel guitar played by Denola Adepoju.

Sunny's 'Syncro System', as he calls his sound, is even more distinct from the older generation of Juju bands because of a strong dash of Pop and Afro-beat. Unlike the older version of Juju which is usually in praise of prominent men, Sunny's lyrics are more about the problems of modern life.

Sunny, whose real name is Sunday Adeniyi, was born in the Ondo State in 1946. He picked up his musical inclinations from his father, who was an organist, and his mother who was in the church choir. He completed his secondary education in Oshogbo and became leader of the school band there. Then he worked for a time with one of the popular travelling comic theatres, that of Moses Olaiya based at Ibadan. From there he moved to Lagos and joined Victor Olaiya's Highlife band, based at the Papingo Club. In 1966 he formed his own band, called the Green Spots, based at the Kue Club in Lagos.

The band's first success came in 1967 with their football song *Challenge Cup*. Since then Sunny has released over a dozen albums, including Nigeria's first double album. He records and releases everything on his own label, Sunny Alade Records, as he does not trust the big companies. He and his band made many tours of North America and Europe, and in Spain Sunny was acclaimed the 'Golden Mercury of Africa'.

On stage Sunny has almost telepathic rapport with his eighteen musicians and is constantly introducing new instruments to the band. He denies that his Juju music is going synthetic. He thinks of it as traditional Yoruba music refined by modern instruments but not changed by them. For instance the local Gonje fiddle has been replaced by the guitar, and the bamboo flute by the clarinet. He's a real believer in musical progress, but progress based on all the traditional cross-rhythms of Africa, not only in the drumming but even in the electric guitars; for each guitar plays its own distinct melodic and rhythmic phrase, all interlacing with each other in a subtle way.

Sunny's ideal in life is to have as beneficial an effect as possible on the largest number of people. He is deeply spiritual and has been a devout Christian since he was seven. He neither smokes nor drinks. He believes that everyone has a special destiny, and that in his case Juju music is his shrine. He even calls his Ariya (Enjoyment) Club a 'church from where my message will reach the masses'.

His music, like all Juju music, has a strong religious and moral bias, and there is a definite overlap of Juju music with the Yoruba hymn music of the Aladura or 'praying' churches, which is often played by electronic guitar bands. Many of Sunny's lyrics are pessimistic predictions of doom, but again this is in the tradition of the revivalist African churches. Sunny hotly denies that his songs are anti-establishment. They are simply about the happenings in society, including its ills.

Sunny Ade at the Lyceum

Sunny can regularly sell 200,000 copies of his albums in Nigeria alone, and recently Island Records (who produced the late Bob Marley) have signed him up and in 1983 organised American and European tours for his African Beats.

Here are two comments on the packed two-and-a-half hour show held at the London Lyceum in January 1983. First from the *New Musical Express* which described the music as 'the most exhilarant yet subtle music heard in London for ages. Interlocking layers of rhythmic patterns create a seamless loop which at one and the same time combine an unforced airy simplicity with a hugely complex range of inflexions and texture.'

And from the *Guardian* newspaper, 'Sunny Ade proved why they call him the "Chairman". He functions less as a star performer than as a conductor orchestrating a series of musical dialogues. The show offered a marked contrast with western song structure and our notions of musical climax. Although the set was divided into songs of varying mood and tempo one had the impression it was all part of the same fabric. Each number ended abruptly — in mid sentence as it were — yet without any feeling of discontinuity. They could have all started at any point and played for ever. Their skills and joyful dedication had the effect of making the panorama of English rock music look jaded and trite.'

In April 1983, on the televised German programme *Rock Palace* (seen by 200 million viewers), the interviewer asked Sunny how he organises and controls his complex, yet laid-back musical structure. Sunny pointed out that he does not control it — rather he orchestrates the parts and each and every musician has a special part to play in the total musical scaffolding. The African Beats' subtle and spacey music always spirals around the main beat, creating ambiguous rhythms difficult to pin down — so different from Western linear music. Even when interviewed, Sunny will never give the opinionated statements expected of a superstar. A master of understatement, he will rather throw the questions back at the interviewer or talk in parables. Because, as in his music, everything is really a question of balancing opposite points of view.

Sunny's growing popularity in the West with his combination of Juju and Pop has encouraged his main rival, Ebeneezer Obey, to change his tune a bit. And after a short period of retirement and renovation Obey has recently come out with a Juju/Rock Fusion that is also becoming popular with European Rock fans, records of which are being released by the New Wave record distributor in London, Rough Trade. He has also recently signed up with Virgin Records.

New trends in Juju

Ebeneezer Obey and Sunny Ade are the two giants of Juju, but there are many Juju bands, around three hundred in the Lagos area alone! Their music now ranges from the more traditional types right through to modern varieties. Many of the old-timers are still playing: I.K. Dairo, Tunde Nightingale and Daniel Akinolu who has been the leader of the Inner Circle Orchestra, since the death of Ayinde Bakare.

Playing in the style pioneered by Ebeneezer Obey are Sir Skiddo and his Mountain Millionaires, a twelve-man band based at Abeokuta. Oladunni Oduguwa or Mummy Juju and her Decency and Unity Orchestra also play in his style, as does Ayinde Barrister who has been in Nigeria's top twenty for some time. Then there is Sir Shina's band from which Segun Adewele broke away to create a more innovative form of Juju.

These days, many Juju musicians are innovators, creating their own 'systems' by incorporating new ideas — and generally taking a lead from Sunny Ade's success. For instance, Prince Adekunle and his Western State Brothers are influenced by Pop and Afro-beat, as is Pick Peters. Then there is Thony Alex who has created a blend he calls the 'Sedico system'. Prince Dele Abiodun is another band leader who has combined Afro-beat and Juju music which he releases on the Olumo label. Up to 1970 he was a Highlife musician, but then formed the Top Hitters Juju band and created his 'Adawa system'. Bob Aladeniyi, originally second in command of Sunny Ade's African Beats, split away in 1975 to form his Jungle Rock Stars which actually recruited Fela's Afro-beat musicians, Edo and Tutu Shorunma.

Juju music quickly absorbs new melodic ideas because musicians use snatches of tunes from anywhere and anyone, incorporating them into a network of criss-crossing melodies. The usual criteria for Copyright law break down with Juju music. For instance, one Juju song copies a phrase from *Somewhere over the Rainbow*, but this is only one of four melodies playing simultaneously and it is used to embellish the main theme, a local melody.

Quite a different current within today's Juju music is the influence of Muslim Yoruba music styles like Apala and Sakara which are less westernised than Juju and use only traditional instruments such as the hand piano, the talking drum, the one-stringed violin and the sakara, a small tambourine made of clay or bamboo. One Juju musician digs this sound so much that he has specialised in fusing Juju and Apala. He is Idowu Animashaun, a man of huge proportions, who formed his Lisabi Brothers in 1966, which is still going strong.

Apala emerged in the middle 1940s as a mixture of traditional Yoruba music and Muslim music from the north. At first it was called 'Area' in Lagos and 'Oshugbo' in Ibadan. The name 'Apala' was coined in 1947 by Haruna Ishola when he formed his Apala Band. Since then he has released scores of singles and albums and dominates the Apala scene.

If anyone imagines that the more traditional music of Apala and Sakara attracts old-fashioned people, one only has to turn to Haruna. In 1979 Haruna Ishola opened the first 24 track studio in Africa, at his home town of Ijebu-Igbo near Ibadan. This is Phono-disc, which makes three out of every ten records pressed in Nigeria, so the indigenous sounds of Apala and Juju are getting first-rate treatment. Sunny Ade himself records there.

The newest craze in the Juju scene is the entry of 'Fuji' music — a Juju sound minus the electric guitars, created by musicians like Ayinde Barrister, Ayinde Kollington and Wahabi Ejire.

So Juju, Fuji and Apala really embrace two worlds, looking forward to technology and backwards to roots.

3 Afro-rock, Osibisa's Criss-cross Rhythms

Rock music, from Elvis to the Beatles, became popular with the youth of Africa during the sixties, and the rock craze was followed by the progressive Rock of Santana, Cream, Jimi Hendrix, Sly and the Family Stone.

At first, young African musicians simply copied Rock and Pop music, but later, especially with the influx of progressive Rock, they began to experiment and fuse their local music with Rock. This is no surprise because, after all, Rock and Roll is based on Black American Rhythm and Blues, the city version of the even earlier Blues, Hollas and work-songs of the Southern plantations, music with roots in Africa.

Osibisa is first and foremost of the Afro-rock bands. They became internationally famous in the early seventies for their criss-cross rhythms which became a craze with Blacks and Whites alike, and anticipated the disco-mania of the mid-seventies. This band, based in London, originally came from Ghana. They ended up making a million pounds for British taxes, for which they were awarded the MBE.

Sylvia Moore at Osibisa's Amsterdam debut

In 1974 Osibisa made their Amsterdam debut in the Paradiso Club, which since 1968 had been the city's hippy hide-out. Actually a disused nineteenth-century Protestant church near the City Theatre, it now houses international restaurants, clubs and disco bars, and glitters with hundreds of sparkling lights. The outer walls of the church have been brightened with blue and red designs, while inside an alternative Paradise, a modern temple, caters for all kinds of young enthusiasts, with billiards, bars, and stalls selling alternative goods, an ever-changing programme of music and theatre workshops, Pop music performances, and the freedom to smoke hash or marijuana with no threat of arrest.

Crowds thronged outside the building. Bouncers apprehensively watched for pushers and trouble-shooters. As the hour approached for the Osibisa happening, the hall suddenly filled up with a mass of people, squeezing into every nook and cranny and pressing close to the stage. Roadies climbed aloft like mariners to adjust stage lights and re-organise a network of cables. Instruments were arranged on the stage. A real palm tree was brought to the front. The flying elephant backcloth was hoisted – a grey elephant with ears shaped like bat-wings, curled tusks, pink, orange, yellow and blue wings. The elephant, which never forgets, is Osibisa's symbol of Africa.

The crack of a thunderstorm, the spit of rain were signs that the long wait for the roadies to get it together, was almost over. The crowds now surged to the edge of the stage, pressing against each other, mesmerised in anticipation. Perched on top of a ten foot high loudspeaker, almost hanging over the stage, I too felt the heat of the rising temperature, a fever which had already blazed across three continents with entranced and amazed followers in its wake.

As the storm and the crowds were about to break, the thunder-claps were interrupted by the impelling criss-cross rhythms of a processional dance. Incessantly, the sounds directed your eyes, your ears, your body –

'Osibisa, Osibisa,' chanted the crowd, and one by one the band emerged in their crazy gear, waving their arms, blowing whistles, chanting exuberantly, beating a wild array of instruments – bells, tambourines, sticks, a Chinese gong, even a dinner bell, and united in one happy, infectious smile.

Teddy Osei, from Kumasi, Ghana, in a shimmering white Indian shirt, blue, red, grey and white striped trousers and silver boots with three-inch heels, moved to the centre front. He took up a position behind the Ashanti atum-pan talking drums and slit drum.

Mac Tontoh, his brother, was close on Teddy's heels with his trumpet, flugel horn, Ashanti cow-horn, his famous Ewe axatse (a beaded gourd rattle) and Ashanti apentemma drums.

Kofi Ayivor, conga king, like Mac naked from the waist up, as Ewes are wont to be, and wearing a traditional Ghanaian cloth wrapped round his waist, was immediately recognisable by his tiny tuft of hair and his muscular stature, as he positioned himself under the palm, behind his congas.

Keyboard wizard, Kiki Gyan, from Cape Coast, Ghana, his wide-brimmed hat as broad as his smile and hardly concealing his translucent eyes, so lively that they

Kofi Ayivor

Teddy Osei and Mac Tontoh

almost pop out of his head. He was wearing a multi-coloured waist-coast, and trousers made of Kente cloth, the Ghanaian traditional silk cloth, woven in a blaze of gold, red and green threads, with the addition of purple for chiefs. The outfit was completed by his checker-board red, white and blue socks, and high-heeled boots.

The inimitable Sol Amarfio, from Accra, Ghana, wearing a skull-cap, African beads and Ghanaian cos-tume, sat behind his drum kit.

The line-up was complete when Camerounian, Jean Mandengue, impressively attired in a shiny blue priest-like robe covered with red designs, picked up his bass guitar, and Paul Golly, born in London of West Indian parents, found his lead guitar.

'Is everybody ready?' Teddy called, in the midst of thunder, rain and lightning. The sounds of the mud-green forest became more insistent — cocks crowing, crickets chirping:

O-SI-BI-SA
Criss-cross rhythms that explode
with happiness.
We're gonna start these happy
vibes right from the root, and
the root is
early one morning in the heart of
AFRICA.

The drums swung into a driving traditional rhythm cycle — men call out and laugh to each other. The morning soundscape was in full swing —

We call this
THE DAWN

The rustle and flutter of birds in distant trees was captured by Kiki's keys — a quavering melody which Teddy's flute echoed, re-echoed higher and higher till it faded away. In came the brass, the flute insistently following each phrase, to close the gaps. Kiki's re-entry was immediately reinforced by a six-beat bell cycle, interlaced and thickened by the rattle rhythm.

But now it was time for the vocalists to show their different colours — calling softly at first, then loudly, and finally reaching a piercing falsetto. The lead guitar took over and drove relentlessly on. Flute, rattle, drums and brass play in turn; then not only brass and flute call and respond to each other's riffs, but Teddy has a con-versation with his own flute before a simulated screech-owl firework whizzes through the air, and, 'Ow!'. Teddy's scream is the cue in the whole ensemble for the final cluster of sounds, asserting that dawn had broken.

The senses have been awakened and there's no way they'll lapse back to the drowsy half-lit world between night and day. Without

24

Sol Amarfio

Kiki Gyan

breathing space, it's straight on, for we're going now — *Woyaya*.

We are going,
Heaven knows where we are going
We know we will.
We will get there
Heaven knows how we will get there
We know we will.

Mac and Sol sing the melody alone, arms round each other's shoulders, swaying to the gentle six-beat rhythm. Mac and Kofi try to outshine each other in playing the axatse rattle — using all parts of their bodies as a sounding board — arms, thighs, chest, head — as Kofi said, 'I play anything with skin on it.' In an outburst of confidence, everyone joins in, grabbing bells, rattles, drums, to beat out the complex, multiple rhythms of a traditional dance. The message was clear.

By now the crowds are emotionally ready for an unadulterated piece of Ghanaian tradition. Mac moves swiftly to the Lobi xylophone, adeptly introducing a Northern rhythm. No need to translate this time — *Let's Do It* — Kelele, in Twi.

Kelele, kelele awo awo kelele.

'Together,' — Teddy shouted — Mac sides with the audience,

Kelele, kelele awo awo kelele.

'Let's hear everybody next time' — but now the public is initiated into the musicians' group and they let go.

Kelele, kelele awo awo kelele.

It's an old Ghanaian technique — drawing the audience in, bringing them as close as you can, then giving it back to them. There's no alternative but to go. Teddy cues in with his hand warbles and mouth percussion and, bang, the rhythm rips on. Inspired, Kofi forsakes his congas, picks up a swish and demonstrates a few scenes from the Ewe Atsiagbevor, a warrior dance, swinging into it with the agbadza movement. Every muscle is responding — his chest is raised and lowered, his shoulder blades almost touch then release, his elbows move back and forward. With bent knees he dances along, co-ordinating this contract and release rhythm of his torso with his breathing rhythm.

By now, it was quite clear that Osibisa were not just a bunch of cheerful loonies who like banging, shaking and scraping assorted bits of wood and skin; nor were they some village musicians out for the night to show they could master some bits and pieces of the Western pop scene.

25

When I first heard the band, I couldn't make out what all the fuss was about. After all, hundreds of musicians were performing the very same music as a matter of course, at various ceremonies all the year round. But it took only one gig to convince me. This was a totally transforming experience, not meant for the ears alone, and which a record could never completely re-create.

What we had here was a thorough mastery of traditional music; a clever understanding of the psychology of involving and winning over the audience; confidence that traditional values and a way of life can be recaptured, renewed and transmitted in a modern mechanised setting; the intelligent harnessing of Western instruments, a wide range of Western popular styles and the acoustic paraphernalia of pop concerts, to create and forge ahead, with the roots as inspiration; and the ability to commercialise African music using the symbols of the West, but leaving the source and the message intact, by bringing in African imagery. All this was the foundation stone of their effervescent philosophy, 'We give you our treasure. Be happy!'

But Osibisa were already rolling on with *Ayiko Bia*, meaning 'well done' in Ga, a perfect example of blending Western instruments with the traditional format, and combining different traditional formulas to get the fullest impact. Starting very simply, the lead singer calls your attention,

Ayiko bia.

in a throaty bass voice. The united response, and shouts of,

Tcha tcha tcha tcha tcha tcha!

lead on to the yodelling sounds Northerners make when possessed. Then — bang — the shock technique of contrasting dynamics, in comes the heavy brass cadence as a bridge to the melody, this time sung an octave higher, by a husky baritone. Throughout, this brass cadence carries the music over different sequences. The lead guitar's jam section is studded by sharp brass thrusts, before and on the beat of each cycle. The melody is re-echoed by the brass section, and then the trumpet improvises on the theme, introducing shades of Masekela. Finally, a pounding traditional rhythm, where the bell and drums in turn shift to accent different beats, while one drum rhythm overlaps, linking cycle to cycle, before the brass bridge cues in the familiar cluster of sounds, bringing the number to a dramatic close.

A myriad of village scenes floated through my mind and I was transported thousands of miles away, before I noticed that Osibisa had left the stage. The audience, too, was transfixed. The aura zones around us all were injected with Osibisa's burning energy. The power of the drums had brought us on to the stage in spirit with them. Real physical and emotional needs were being satisfied. We were not prepared to terminate the affair abruptly, and return to the cold before the climax had been reached. Our idols must return. We chanted, whistled and called with one voice — a Black and White crowd, almost half of them were Europeans, mainly Dutch and the rest were people of African descent from Surinam and the Dutch Antilles.

Kofi was persuaded to come on stage. He carried a broomstick covered with hundreds of bottle tops. Beating the stick on the ground and using his voice as a percussion instrument, he set a complex rhythm going which caught on backstage. Soon they were all back.

'Are you all happy?' asks Teddy.

'Yeah!'

'Then everybody scream.'

Now our cries cued in Osibisa's *Happy Children*, and in no time everyone was dancing about, clapping their hands and joining in the chorus.

Finally, Osibisa burst into *Fire*, a thumping number which had become a signature tune for Manchester United Football Club. Indeed the wild, almost frenzied enthusiasm had something in common with the football ground.

By this time the transformation was complete. A small lad stood on the stage engrossed. People had stopped dancing and, as in Ghana, moved close to the stage with eyes wide open, staring at the band, pulled in, magnetised and satisfied. The desert had come to life, even though the mirage was about to disappear. Paradise was an indelible memory.

Osibisa's beginnings

How could these extraordinary developments ever have got off the ground in the musical and social climate of the late sixties? At the end of the 1950s, both Teddy and Mac were playing in two of

Ghana's most popular Highlife bands. Teddy had formed The Comets in 1958 which rocketed to fame in West Africa after their recording of *Pete Pete* became a local hit. Mac had joined The Uhuru, in the early days known as The Broadway Band, and also established in 1958, at Takoradi by Sam Obote, a Nigerian.

But Teddy became fed up with the local scene not really going anywhere. As far as trends in the Western music industry were concerned the 'roots' were virtually non-existent. Why couldn't the whole range of Black-derived Western Pop music be broken down into the original African formula and not the other way round? The kind of musical versatility expected of the African musician in the entertainment business should surely make it possible to create a cultural confluence between the old Folk tunes (with their own style of rhythm, melody and timbre qualities, the rich pulsating rhythms, the instrumental variety, the creative energy of Africa), and the various facets of popular music as an overlayer (Gospel, Blues, Jazz, Bossanova, Soul, Funk and so on). For as Teddy pointed out, 'Soul and Reggae derive from Africa, so why don't people recognise the original first?'

It was this rather stagnant state of affairs which made Teddy decide to go to London in 1962. In Ghana, his job after leaving technical building college was as a building inspector, but music was his first love. Born in Kumasi, as a young boy he had already learned to play Ashanti percussion instruments used for various ceremonies, such as the Ashanti atumpan drums. At school, of course, he played drums for the brass band. Later he picked up the sax by chance, and then the flute. After playing in big name bands like the Star Gazers, with drummer and percussionist, Sol Amarfio, he led his own band, The Comets, in which his brother, Mac Tontoh, also played. The Comets, scored many singles hits throughout West Africa in the late 1950s, the last one *Pete Pete* being simultaneously number one in Ghana, Nigeria and Sierra Leone.

In London, he found that it was not easy to start playing music. 'I washed plates in hotels for six months and bought my own saxophone. But no musician was interested in me, so I had to convince them of my worth. Later I got some Africans together and we started playing for Africans during the summer'.

The Nkrumah government gave him a scholarship to study music at a London school, a training which he later found useful when it came to arranging for his own group. After playing in a few nightclubs, he formed Cat's Paws, which veered towards soul music, as a means of getting work. After a residency in Zurich's Beat Club and a three-month exposure at a 1969 festival in Tunis, Cat's Paws returned to London. 'We got so much inspiration that we discovered we had to put more into African music.' Teddy brought Mac Tontoh and Sol Amarfio over to London. After Teddy left Ghana in 1962, Mac had spent one year with a military dance band, playing at top state functions, and then joined the Uhurus, the first big band of its kind in Africa. In addition to the styles they were playing in 1967, their music also ranged from Glen Miller to Charlie Parker. Sol, born in Accra, was playing maraccas, bongos and congas with local bands at the age of twelve. When he was sixteen, he joined the Rhythm Aces, then the Star Gazers. In 1968 he started playing the full, conventional drum kit.

After an offer to record a soundtrack to a film set in Africa, Teddy started to work on the Osibisa sound, along with four West Africans and two West Indians — later to be joined by a third West Indian. The group included his brother, Mac Tontoh, who had learned to play the Lobi xylophone from Lobi musicians who had settled in his village. In addition, he plays assorted traditional percussion, including drums and Ewe instruments, such as the gangogui (double bell of welded iron) and the axatse (beaded calabash rattle). Other instruments he plays are trumpet and flugel horn. Lofty Lasisi Amao, a Nigerian, playing tenor sax, baritone sax and congas, had also come to London with Mac and Sol. They were joined by Spartacus R from Grenada, on bass guitar and assorted percussion, Wendell Richardson from Antigua, on lead guitar and vocals, and Robert Bailey from Trinidad on organ, piano and timbales. Needless to say, it comes as first nature to all members of the group to play percussion and sing, drawing on the African traditions which had been handed down to them.

The name of the group was changed to Osibisa, which in Twi means 'criss-cross rhythms that explode with happiness'. Richard

Williams recalled his first meeting with Osibisa:

6 At that time, Osibisa had nothing — except their instruments, their talent, and their twofold love: for their music and for each other. They were totally unknown, just starting out in one of the world's most competitive arenas.

They played for me that afternoon, and that tiny, cramped room filled up with the sound of joy. To say that I was transfixed would be a massive understatement, and I left the place, a couple of hours later, reeling with the delight of stumbling across something very important indeed.

Soon after that meeting, they were unleashed on the British public, and the effect was astonishing. They took audiences who'd grown used to sitting on the floor and marvelling at superfast lead guitarists, grabbed them by the scruff of the neck and made them dance. They'd come out of the blue: four West Africans and three West Indians, most of whom has been close to starvation for a year or more. They were hungry, and that hunger was plain in their music. It showed itself in an energy and urgency long lost and forgotten by most European musicians, and suddenly audiences everywhere were responding. 9

(*Woyaya* sleeve notes)

In 1970 Osibisa took off, after releasing their first single, *Music for Gong-Gong* and began to get popular at clubs like Ronnie Scott's, the Roundhouse and the Country Club — all in London.

A number of musicians has passed through the group since its early days. Originally on bass there was Spartacus from Grenada, followed by Fred Coker and then Mike Odumosu (both from Nigeria). Del Richardson from Trinidad was their lead guitarist for a long time. Then on congas were Lofty Lassissi Amoah from Nigeria and Kofi Ayivor from Ghana. And on keyboards Robert Bailey from Trinidad and Kiki Gyan from Ghana.

From 1971, first on the MCA and then the Bronze label, they released a string of albums and singles: Albums like *Osibisa*, *Heads*, *Happy Children*, *Welcome* and *Black Magic Night*; Singles that got into the British Top Ten, like *Sunshine Day*, *Dance the Body Music* and the *Coffee Song*.

However, in the mid-seventies in England, with the decline of Rock music and the appearance of Disco and New Wave, Osibisa's Afro-rock also suffered. So the band simply packed their bags and spent most of their time outside Britain on international tours of Australia, the East, Europe and Africa, where they had massive followings.

Of course the one country they kept going back to was Ghana, where they became a constant source of inspiration for the youth. Even in the villages their music was a success, especially their *Music for Gong-Gong*, which became a standard amongst the rural guitar bands. They also put on big shows in Ghana, like the one they did at the El Wak Stadium in Accra in 1977. They brought over heavy amplification with them.

Ironically they represented, along with other artists, the Black and African communities resident in Britain at the Black Arts Festival, FESTAC, held in Nigeria in 1977. They were also invited to the celebrations connected with the independence of Zimbabwe and the inauguration of the Cultural Ministry, and played to a crowd of 25,000 people in the capital. They are getting more and more back to their roots, and in 1980 released, on their own Flying Elephant label, the old South African hit *Pata-Pata*.

Osibisa with Remi Kabaka at the Royal Albert hall

28

Ginger Baker

Joni Haastrup

4 Afro-rock Catches On

Osibisa isn't the only group to have influenced the growth of Rock in Africa. In Nigeria another stimulus in this direction has come from British drummer, Ginger Baker, who played with two of Britain's top Rock bands of the sixties, Cream and Blind Faith.

Ginger Baker's influence

In 1970 Ginger, by then running a band called Airforce, visited Nigeria. He travelled via Ghana where he stayed for a time with the famous Ghanaian Afro-jazz drummer Guy Warren, or Kofi Ghanaba as he now calls himself. In Nigeria Ginger was given a big welcome by Afro-beat king Fela Aníkúlápo-Kuti and they jammed together at the Afro-spot. Also playing was one of Nigeria's oldest established Pop groups, the Clusters, and Ginger was so impressed by their leader, Joni Haastrup, that he took him back to England to play organ for Airforce for eighteen months.

The rest of Clusters: Berkley Jones, Laolu Akins, Mike Odumosu and Bob Cole, joined up with Tunde Kuboye and the Swiss-Nigerian flute player Tee Mac to form the Afro-collection — a band influenced by the progressive freak Rock of Jimi Hendrix, Santana, Sly and the Family Stone and Blood Sweat and Tears. Tee Mac's Afro-collection was based at the Batakoto Club in Lagos, set up by Ginger Baker and a Nigerian partner.

When Airforce broke up in 1971, Ginger returned to Nigeria across the desert, in a Range Rover. At his club he was so taken with Afro-collection, that he asked Berkley, Laolu and Tunde to join a new band he wanted to form called Salt.

The other members of the band were two European musicians Steve Gregory and Bud Beadle and two Nigerian vocalists called the Lijadu Sisters. Salt was outdoored in Nigeria in 1972 at a huge show at the Kakadu Club in Lagos. Another Afro-rock band was launched then, a six-piece group called Ofo and the Black Company. After this show Salt went to the Olympic Jazz Festival and then on to an American tour.

But Ginger's effect on the Nigerian Rock scene didn't stop at moving Nigerian musicians around the world. He also helped set up Africa's first 16 track recording studio, the Associated Recording Company, or ARC, studio at Ikeja. He put a film together which featured himself, Fela and the Africa 70, the Afro-collection, Segun Bucknor and the artist-musician Twin Seven Seven.

Mono Mono and BLO

The Ginger Baker—Afro-collection dialogue led to the formation of the most important rock groups in Nigeria such as Mono Mono, which means 'lightning', formed in 1971 by Joni Haastrup after his tour with Ginger's Airforce. Mono Mono's early hit record was a Haastrup composition called *Lidalu*. BLO was formed when bassist Mike Odumosu, drummer Laolu Akins and guitarist Berkley Jones returned from the European—American tour with Salt. The name of the band, BLO, is taken from the initials of these three musicians, and it released a number of successful Afro-rock numbers like *Native Doctor* and *Preacher Man*.

The Funkees

Another of the first Nigerian Afro-rock bands, but this time from the east of the country, was the Funkees, formed during the height of Nigerian Civil War in 1969. The band's leader was Jake Solo who had previously been with the Hykkers, a Pop group from Enugu. The Funkees combined pure Funk with the local Igbo Atilogwu beat, and their first hit single in Nigeria was *Onyemanya*, released in 1971, followed by *Akula* and *Dancing Time*, both released on the EMI Nigeria label.

Afro-rock in Ghana

In Ghana, the main stimulus to Afro-rock besides Osibisa, was the Soul to Soul concert held in Accra in 1971, which featured the Latin-rock of Santana. This gave an incentive to a whole generation of young pop musicians to experiment with Rock combined with their own rhythms, just as Carlos Santana had done with Latin-American music and Rock.

The Aliens pop band in Accra went psychedelic, due to the influence of freak guitarist Jimmy Hendrix. They released an EP of music that combined Jimmy's guitar style with an African backing. They were followed shortly after by a group called Hedzolleh, meaning 'freedom'. On stage, they were more African than Osibisa. The group was based at the famous Napoleon Club in Accra.

Another top Ghanaian Rock band in the mid-seventies was Cosmic Boombaya which was based at Wato's Club, overlooking one of Accra's busiest roundabouts. Yet another was the Q Masters, based in Ghana but mainly composed of Sierra Leonese musicians. They stayed in Kumasi for several years where they expounded the cross-beat, a combination of Rock and the rhythms of the secret Poro society of Sierra Leone.

All over English-speaking Africa, Rock became popular. In South Africa it became a craze with the youth in the townships like Soweto. In East Africa, too, there are bands like Matato of Kenya, which plays in the style of BLO, and Ofege, and the six-piece Rock band Makonde formed in 1977.

Afro-rock goes abroad

As a consequence of the Black and White fusion, many of the African bands that play Afro-rock have ended up in the States and Europe, leading to a great deal of cross-fertilisation in the international rock scene. The members of Afro-collection, who joined Ginger, and Ofo and the Black Company, ended up in the States. The Funkees also went abroad to Britain in 1973 and later Jake Solo played with Osibisa, as did Mike Odumosu of BLO.

The Ghanaian bands Hedzolleh

Ojah playing at London Dingwalls in 1979

and Boombaya also made the pilgrimage abroad, to the States and Britain respectively, and both stayed, as did the Sierra Leonese band Super Combo which was resident in London for a time. Also in London is the Afro/Jazz/Rock fusion group from South Africa called Jabula, and Ojah, which was actually formed in London by the Ghanaian bassist Nana Tsiboe and the English musician Willie Stallibros (originally with the Rock group Chilli Willi and the Red Hot Peppers).

Then there have been many individual African musicians working in the American and European rock scenes. One of the first was the Ghanaian conga player Speedy Acquaye who worked with Georgie Fame and the Blue Flames in the sixties. The Nigerian percussionist Remi Kabaka is another who has worked with Ginger Baker, Stevie Winwood and Mick Jagger. Another Nigerian, Gaspar Lawal, has worked with Ginger's Airforce and with the Rolling Stones. In fact the idea for the popular Beatles' song *Obladi Oblada* was given to them by Jimmy Scott, the Nigerian Conga player.

Eddie Quansah, Ghana's Black trumpet, also left home and worked as a session musician in Europe for many years. He finally got the money from Island Records to return home and produce a top-selling Afro-rock album called *Che Che Kule*.

Another Ghanaian rock musician, who was actually brought up in Britain, is Kris Bediako. He returned home in the mid-seventies to form his Band called Bediako which became very popular.

Speedy Acquaye (wearing hat) and Louis Moholo

White rock goes to Africa

White Rock musicians are now going to Africa to play and record. Ginger is one and another is Paul McCartney whose band Wings recorded *Band on the Run* in Lagos in the mid-seventies. More recently, in 1981, Mick Fleetwood of Fleetwood Mac visited Ghana. He came with two American Rock musicians Todd Sharpe and George Hawkins, plus twelve tons of equipment and a 16 track recording studio with which they recorded their album *The Visitor*. Fleetwood Mac's big hit of the sixties *Black Magic Woman* had become fantastically popular in Ghana, especially when Santana

did a version of it. This helped blow the creative lid off the local Afro-rock scene.

Afro-rock today – Nigeria

Today Afro-rock is still a powerful force in Africa, in spite of the demise of Rock in the West, and without doubt the main centre of the African Rock industry is Nigeria with its modern multi-track studios and the release of twenty million records a year. The top Nigerian Rock artist at the moment is the young Chris Okotie who has been a teenage heart-throb since 1980 when he released his first album *I Need Someone*. It sold over 100,000 copies in six months and so earned Chris a gold disc. He comes from the Bendel State and is a law student at the University of Enugu. He sings rather like an African Bob Dylan, and is influenced by James Brown (he was a JB freak in the early seventies), Hot Chocolate and Cat Stevens. On the cover of his second album, on the Phonodisc label called *Just for You*, he is dressed as a knight in shining armour, much to the delight of the Nigerian damsels.

Another top Rock and Pop group is Bongos Ikwue and his Groovies. He started professional singing in 1967 and his first hit came in 1974 with *Sitting on the Beach* sung in the style of Otis Redding. Then he released *Otachik-pokpo* in his own Indoma language and in 1977 and 1978 was awarded two gold discs for his two albums *Still Searching* and *Something Good*. Bongos sings everything from Rock and Reggae to funky Calypsos and

Highlife in his distinctive soft, gravelly voice. His harmonies are reminiscent of the Everly Brothers.

Another Nigerian pop star who has just risen to fame is Tony Grey and his Black Kings. His *Gospel of Ozzimba* could be termed Pop Highlife. His album *Please Don't Leave Me*, for instance, is sung in English. He uses a moog-synthesiser, but keeps to West Africa's traditional twelve-beat cycle.

Not all of Nigeria's Pop stars are men. One important exception is the actress and singer Patti Boulaye, who won the television *New Faces* competition in 1978 and then released her first album called *Patti Boulaye*. This included ballads, Rock and Roll, and Soul. Her second album *Music Machine* is more Disco oriented and was the soundtrack to a film.

Most of Nigeria's first Rock artists are still active. Tee Mac is now a music promoter and has his own record label called SKJ Records. Mike Odumosu likewise has set up his own record company in Nigeria which has released an album called *Sunshine in Africa*. He is currently playing with the Gonzales group in the States. Jake Solo is back in Nigeria and has decided to revive the Hykkers, one of Nigeria's first Pop bands. BLO is still around and has done the backing for another female Nigerian Rock vocalist called Christine Essien, whose album *Give me a Chance*, was released on the Decca label in 1981.

Afro-rock today – Ghana

Despite the serious economic situation, causing many musicians

Chris Okotie

to spend time abroad, Ghana too has many Afro-rock bands today, such as Bob Pinado from Winneba, whose Sonobete dance was a hit in Ghana in the late sixties. After this, like so many others, he had to spend many years abroad and released top tunes, like *The Girl with the Guitar-shaped Body*, in Germany. The famous Ghanaian vocalist Pat Thomas has also spent a lot of time in Germany. He was originally with the Sweet Bands run by the Tema Food Complex which played everything from Rock to Highlife. He later teamed up with Smart Nkansa's band Sunsum (soul) whose *Sunsum Beat* is funky Rock. Also based in Tema is the young singer Eric Agyeman of the Sweet Talks, who combines Highlife and Pop. Another of Ghana's leading vocalists, Jeff Tagoe, spends most of his time in Nigeria — but when in Ghana is backed by another super pop highlife group called Vis-à-Vis.

Afro-rock today – French-speaking Africa

Even the French-speaking countries of Africa are now producing their own distinct blend of African Rock and Pop, with the emphasis on the voice and front-line instruments. Cameroons' Manu Dibango for instance is a master of Rhythm and Blues, Rock's progenitor. Some of Pierre Akendengue's (the blind guitarist from Gabon) songs are main-line Afro-French Pop — as are many of the songs of Ivorian artists like Pierre Amande, Ernesto Dje Dje and Aicha Koje.

Rock hasn't only affected the urban music of Africa — it has also penetrated deep into the tradi-

Bongos Ikwue

tional guitar band music. The line-up of a typical guitar band today is almost identical to that of a Rock group: lead, rhythm and bass guitars, trap-drums and sometimes an organ. In addition the guitar bands use congas and a percussion section, but then many of today's Rock bands also include a rhythm section.

A circuit completed

So whether it's the Juju music of Sunny Ade and Idowu Animashaun, the highlife bands of African Brothers and Eddie Donkor, or the up-dated griot music of the Ambassadors Dance Band of Mali, they are all fusions of African music and Rock, or the Pop music that has grown out of it.

It's strange to think that Rock is now thriving in Africa under so many guises. But it is a circuit completed: African work songs became Rhythm and Blues, this in turn became White Rock and Roll and finally ended up back in the African mainstream.

33

5 Afro-disco

The disco dance craze and the maxi single burst into the mid-seventies at a time when Pop fans in the West had stopped dancing and were sitting, listening in stoned-out passivity to the psychedelic music of rock superstars. It was the cross-rhythms of Osibisa that first got them on their feet, until this band's natural rhythms were eclipsed by Black American Soul and Funk, mechanised into Disco by German musicians-cum-computer-operators like Kraftwerk. A similar German band, Munich Machine, backs Donna Summers at exactly 154 beats per minute. Boney M also first hit the jackpot in Germany.

This German man-machine fusion swept the world and, for a time, amongst the youth in Africa, it looked as if Disco-mania was going to swamp local music completely. Many bands copied this music. The local live music and open-air clubs dwindled, and everybody started crowding into dark and stuffy discotheques.

Since the initial knock-out, shock-wave of super-produced disco, African musicians at home and abroad have been on the offensive, creating their own distinct blends of African Disco — something that is surely needed, especially as there is a tendency in disco to drift into the watered-down and mediocre musak of Euro-Pop groups like Abba.

Irresistible Disco

It would be impossible to mention all the African Disco bands and artists as so many groups have been influenced by this irresistible dance-music. Osibisa experimented with it before their *Pata Pata* release of 1980, and several ex-Osibisa members have continued in the Disco line — Kiki Gyan, for example, the Ghanaian keyboards player, who has recorded with drummer Glen Warren, and Glen's dad, the famous Guy Warren of Ghana. Likewise congaist Kofi Ayivor is now producing Disco music. Then there is the Nigerian bassist Jake Solo who recently released a Disco record in Europe called *Boogie Legs* and in 1981 in Nigeria released *Shake your Ya Ya* on the Tabansi label. Jake's first band was the Pop group based at Nsukka University called Hykkers that played Beatles-type music. He then joined up with the Afro-rock groups the Funkees and Osibisa and stayed in England for ten years altogether. Since 1977, with his *Coming Back Home* album, made when he visited FESTAC, he has had the intention of returning home to Enugu to add his professional touch to the music scene there.

Other Nigerian musicians are also producing a lot of Disco material. Sonny Okosun is creating a kind of Disco Ozzidi music. The drummer Remi Kabaka, released *Funky Lagos* in 1981. Then Nigeria's top female pop singer Patti Boulaye made her *Music Machine* album.

A Ghanaian musician who has had some Disco works pressed, is the trumpeter Eddie Quansah. He spent a long time as a session musician in London and then signed a contract with Island Records to make his catchy funky-highlife album *Che Che Kulay*, released simultaneously in Europe and Africa in 1978. Then there is the Ghanaian athlete turned musician, Sidiku Buari, who spent some time in the States and returned home in 1979 after releasing his *Disco Soccer* album.

In 1980 the World Disco Championship, which involved 14,000 contestants, was won by the creative dancing of the thin and lanky South African Godfrey Raseroka.

Akie Deen

An African producer who created a different mode out of the unstoppable influence of Disco music, is Akie Deen, a Sierra Leonian based in London, who has moved in a big way into the Afro-Caribbean Disco market that has grown up in the last few years. One of the effects of the international Disco fever was the updating of Calypsos, Meringues, Sambas and Rumbas by artists like Ed Watson and Mighty Sparrow. Lord Kitchener, whose Calypsos were so popular in the fifties has also had a new lease of life and his *Sugar Bum Bum* was a major success in the late seventies and was played at all West Indian parties.

Akie Deen simply moved into this field with his Disco versions of Sierra Leonese Meringues and Ghanaian Highlifes, calling his sound 'Discolypso' to avoid the prefix 'Afro' which he believes is commercially overplayed.

Akie is a friendly, larger-than-life person who is constantly on the go.

Bunny Mack (1) and Akie Deen (r)

He knows practically all the African musicians around in the UK and many come to record as session musicians for his rapidly expanding Afro-disco productions. Ironically, after spending ten years in England and gaining some success there, including several chart hits, his music has now really caught on back in Africa. The radio stations are constantly playing his productions, especially the Ivory Coast Radio. In Nigeria one of his records won a gold award in 1981 and he is now busily opening up distribution in East Africa and Zimbabwe.

Akie, who was born in Freetown in 1947, first became interested in music production when he was Social Secretary of the Sierra Leonese Students' Union in England. It was in 1972 when he had his first opportunity, when he helped organise an eight-week tour of Sierra Leone's top guitar band, the Afro Nationals. He was also involved with their first releases, the two singles *Dem Kick* and *Wondemuyie*.

Even though these records were popular back home in West Africa, in England there were problems, as he explains:

> It was with great difficulty that I got the first shop in London to take even ten records. Also I had no car and had to put the records in a friend's car. We used to attend parties and ask the DJ to play them in order to sell them.

Then in 1973 Akie arranged a tour of the UK for Ghana's top guitar band, the African Brothers, and recorded two songs by them, including the popular *Maria* based on a Congolese rhythm. At the first pressing only 250 were made. Akie described how hard it was initially:

> At first I faced great difficulty and I couldn't sell them as the shops wouldn't accept them. That was until I convinced Steve Barnard, a DJ on Radio London's Reggae Time, to play them on the air. Then I got requests for boxes of 25 from shops who had only taken a single copy. In one week I got through 500.

In 1974 Akie produced two bands. One was Super Combo with whom he made the highlife meringue *Woko*. The other group was the Funkees from Nigeria. The first album by this Afro-rock band was called the *Point of No Return*, and was jointly produced by Akie and Dan Jegede.

The following year, members of the Afro Nationals, under the name Sabannah 75 came to London again and, helped by Akie, released the three singles, *Susanna*, *Konko* and *Carry On*. They all became big hits back in Sierra Leone. The band returned yet again in 1977, and Akie released a twelve-inch single version of Rokafil Jazz's *Sweet Mother* with them, under the registered Afro-disco name of Wagadugu.

Miatta Fahnbulleh

In 1977 Akie started working with Liberia's top female vocalist Miatta Fahnbulleh, who recorded two traditional songs in Disco style with him. *Amo Sakee Sa* and the Reggae *Kokolioko*. In spite of her international upbringing (her father was a diplomat in Liberia,

Sierra Leone, Kenya and Britain), her music is rooted in the Liberian culture — a mixture of African, Afro-American, West Indian and European influences. She describes her music as African music.

> It comes from Africa but it embraces the whole world. As far as I see my music, it is to deliver everything that is happening in the so-called commercial music of today, but emphasising the roots as it is.

And she is in a good position to add an international touch to the local Liberian Folk music, as her travelling continued even after leaving school. For a time she worked for the *Voice of Kenya* and then went to the States to study journalism. While in New York she sang at the famous Apollo Theatre in Harlem, studied at the American Musical and Dramatic Academy, and worked with the Negro Ensemble Theatre of New York and with Duke Pearson of Blue Note Records.

She returned home in 1973 to appear as a guest artist at President Tolbert's inauguration, then returned again in 1974 to discover she was a star there. So she toured West Africa with a Sierra Leonian band usually resident in Lagos called Baranta. After that, she worked with the South African trumpeter Hugh Masekela and with Nigerian artists like Jimi Solanke and Remi Kabaka. In 1977 she represented Liberia at the Black Arts Festival in Lagos.

The same year she went back to England and worked with a number

Jake Solo of the Funkees

Remi Kabaka

36

of musicians and producers — Jah Bunny of Matumbi and, of course, Akie Dean of Afro-discs.

More successes for Akie Deen

After Miatta's Disco successes, Akie continued to release his evolving Discolypso sound. There was the single *Tumba*, and *Carolina* by Addy Foster Jones who works for Sierra Leone television. Teddy Davies did a version of Lord Kitchener's popular *Just a Little Bit*. Akie also produced a single by Nigeria's Jake Solo, licensed by Pye.

But the big breakthrough into the Afro-Caribbean Disco market came in 1979 with the release of *Easy Dancing* by Wagadugu, followed by *Discolypso* and *Funny Lady* by Cecil Bunting McCormack, or Bunny Mack from Sierra Leone.

In January 1980 this was followed by Bunny Mack's first entry into the British pop-charts called *Love you Forever*, which got to number five in the UK disco charts and 76 in the singles charts. This was also a hit song in West Africa, and in Nigeria it earned a gold disc as it sold over 100,000 copies there on the Tabansi label.

Akie followed this huge success by even more Disco singles like *Weakness for your Sweetness* by Jimmy Senyah from Barbados which reached number 25 in the British Disco charts and, when released by Scorpion Records in France, got into the French hit-parade as well.

Other artists whom Akie is producing include Emmanuel Rentoz

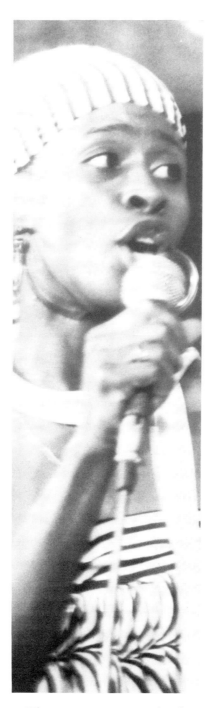

Miatta Fahnbulleh of Liberia

a keyboards player from Ghana, the singer Nina da Costa from the West Indies, Yvonne Mobambo from South Africa, Leon Charles from Barbados and the operatic and folk singer from Nigeria, Martha Ulaeto.

Akie also organised tours of Nigeria for Bunny Mack to co-incide with Bunny Mack's new release *Supa Frico*. But let's give Akie the last word on his music.

'I've developed a new sound called Discolypso, which is a fusion of Calypso and African rhythms. This beat, starting off with Bunny Mack's record *Discolypso* progressed to *Let me Love you Forever*, which made an impact on the UK market. And I'm going to continue developing that sound until subsequently African music is accepted. It's just a matter of time.'

So the story of African Disco is a strange one. The roots of Disco lie in Black American Soul and Funk — Soul king James Brown admits that he got some of his dance rhythms from East Africa. When it became computerised into Disco it swept everything aside. And when introduced to Africa it brought in the idea of dancing in dark, enclosed rooms; quite different from the normal practice of dancing in open-air dance halls and, in the case of traditional music, by moonlight. At first Disco had a negative effect on the local African dance scene, but today a new type of Afro-disco musicians and producers has appeared who are now even beginning to affect the Western Disco market.

John and Victor Uwaifo recording a track for an album

6 Victor Uwaifo, the Guitar-boy

Victor Uwaifo is one of the most dynamic of Africa's modern musicians. He has released over one hundred singles and a dozen albums since he formed his Melody Maestros in 1965. His music has a driving beat based on the local folk music from the Bendel state of Nigeria, merged with a modern touch.

It all started in 1966 when he and his band released three smash hits on the Phonogram label. These singles were *Sirri-Sirri*, *Joromi* and *Guitar-boy*. *Joromi*, based on the story of a legendary hero of Benin City, was so popular that it earned him Africa's first Gold Disc Award in 1969. *Joromi* also became the name for one of the bright African cloth designs.

Since then, Victor has become so famous that the students of Nsukka University knighted him 'Sir' Victor Uwaifo, a name that has stayed with him ever since.

The Melody Maestros have made many international tours. They represented Nigeria at the Black Arts Festival held in Dakar in 1966, and played at the Algerian Arts Expo in 1969 and the 1970 World Expo in Japan. They have also toured in the USA, Europe and Russia.

I first met Victor in 1975 when recording a track on Victor's *Laugh and Cry* album, released by Black Bell.

That Christmas I joined him in Benin City and toured eastern Nigeria with his group. In Benin, I stayed at Victor's hotel on the outskirts of town, called the Joromi Hotel, after his first smash-hit. The band was based at a newly opened air-conditioned night-club he owned in the centre of town, known as the Club 400.

A typical show would start with the ten-man Melody Maestros warming up with some Soul and Pop numbers. Then in would come Victor wearing some spectacular clothes he designed himself, and he would take over. A one-man show ensued, with Victor dancing, singing and playing various instruments, like the flute or the organ, which he sometimes plays with his chin. But his main instrument is the guitar and he is a wizard at it, leaving everyone spellbound, with his amazing *Joromi* solo.

When playing, Victor is backed by two midgets who play clips and maraccas. Sometimes the two midgets move backwards and forwards across the stage, darting in between Victor's legs. One of them, King Pago, was with the famous Lagos-based Bobby Benson's Dance Band during the fifties.

Bicycle spokes as frets

Victor was born in 1941 in Benin City, the ancient capital of the Benin Empire. All his family were musical and he became interested in the guitar.

❝ I used to go around to the palm-wine guitarist downtown. The most famous of these guitarists in Benin was We-We, who had been a soldier during the Second World War. So I made a crude guitar myself, with high-tension wires for strings and bicycle spokes for frets. I begged one of the guitarists to teach me how to tune the guitar and he said he wouldn't, unless I bought him a jug of palm-wine. ❞

Even though his father played accordion, he did not like the idea of Victor playing the guitar, associated as it was with drunkenness.

I found my home-made guitar very inferior, so I decided to buy one for myself. But it was difficult as I didn't know how to put it to my father. He would never agree. But I earned my one guinea and bought a second-hand guitar. The first time my father saw me playing it he seized it and threatened to destroy it. But my mother saved it.

Victor left Benin and went to secondary school at Saint Gregory's in Lagos. In his spare time joined the well-established Highlife dance band of Victor Olaiya. Then in 1962 he won a scholarship to the Yaba College of Technology where he spent his time on three main interests: studying in the morning, wrestling and athletics in the afternoon, and playing with E.C. Arinze's Highlife band at the Kakadu Club in the evenings.

In 1964 he joined the Nigerian Television Service as a graphic artist. It was at this time that he first began to put his own band together.

Colours in sound

The first sound Victor created was the 'Akwete' beat, and his first three hit singles were based on that rhythm. As he explains, it was his knowledge of art that helped him create this, by using colours to represent musical notes.

It was at art school that I discovered colours in sound, and sound in colours. I was able to transpose them so that Do, the strongest note, was black, Ray was red, Me was blue, Fa was green. So,

a neutral colour and sound was white, La was yellow and Ti violet. But the whole change came when I transposed the colours of Akwete cloth, hand-woven cloth made in eastern Nigeria. It is a very beautiful cloth and you will see that different colours recur, creating a moving rhythm of colour. When I interpreted this, it gave the "Akwete" sound.

By the late sixties he was fusing this Akwete beat with Pop influences.

I developed the "Shadow" which was a link between the Akwete and the Twist. The Shadow lasted a year and I made an LP of it, but then Soul came, and I started losing fans, so I had to bridge the gap. I had to create a rhythm similar to Soul as well as my original sound. This was "Mutaba".

Some critics have condemned Victor for his modernising influences, but Victor has an answer.

They fail to see that the foundation of my music is very cultural, as demonstrated in the beat and the lyrics. The fact that I use modern instruments to produce my sound has not altered the basic character of the music, otherwise we might as well argue that a historian writing ancient history with modern tools, like a Parker pen and paper, is a farce. The tools he uses to write history will not alter the facts and dates of the book. We have experimentation and evolution of ancient African cultures and my music is no exception to this.

But in fact Victor has based much of his music on the pure rhythms of Benin like 'Ekassa'.

It was a royal dance performed during the coranation of a new king. Some people thought it an abomination to hear "Ekassa" while the king was still alive, but I didn't mind them as the first tune was a brilliant hit and others followed.

Sasakossa was another of Victor's styles based on tradition:

There was a time when the Benin Kingdom was overpowered. It was when the King of England sent explorers to Africa to trade with the King of Benin. But the King had an important festival and said he would not grant the British an audience. But they were stubborn to come and were intercepted and killed. A few managed to escape to England where they were reinforced and came back for revenge. It was then that Benin was almost completely destroyed and the Oba (King) went into hiding. The King had an orderly called Sasakossa who used to sing in a popular way to warn him that there was danger and it was not safe to come out of hiding. So that's where I got the rhythm for Sasakossa.

Never one to stay still for long, Victor has recently begun to experiment with combinations of reggae and the forceful beat of Benin. Victor has a genius for linking up old and new, blended with a touch of his own unique and individual brilliance.

Kofi Ayivor

7 The Drums of Kofi Ayivor

For the last twenty years Kofi Ayivor's drumming has been heard all over the world — even in the Arctic circle — and Kofi has backed many top musicians and groups such as E.T. Mensah, Miles Davis, Eddie Grant, Alexis Korner, Osibisa and even a Turkish band. In fact Kofi is so well travelled that he has got through fifteen passports.

He recently married and decided it was time to settle down, start producing his own albums and set up his own record company. This company, Ivory Records, will be based in Nigeria, his home, Ghana, and The Netherlands. For Kofi has left the United Kingdom and moved to The Netherlands with his Surinam wife.

Mastering the rhythms

But let's go back to the start of Kofi's chequered musical career. One of Kofi's parents was Ghanaian, the other Togolese, and he spent the first ten years of his life at the town of Gusau in Nigeria's Sokoto State. In 1949 his family returned to Deinu in Ghana, on the border with Togo. It was here, in the Ewe region of West Africa, so famous for its knowledge of cross-rhythms, that Kofi first started up on drums. His uncle, who was the master-drummer of Deinu, was his first teacher. It was on this solid foundation that he has been able to build up and master over 45 drumming styles from all over Africa.

Kofi's father, who was a retailer, hated the idea of his son becoming a drummer, as he wanted him to be a doctor. But Kofi was so keen to play drums, that he would walk a twenty-mile round trip to see top Ghanaian bands, like the Black Beats and E.T. Mensah's Tempos, play in the neighbouring town of Lome. And of course he would join in.

> Sometimes I would play the maraccas. If the maraccas player was in love with some girl and he was gone, I would take over.

Kofi joins the Tempos

When he finished school in 1959, Kofi went to Accra and got a job as a lift operator. He decided to try his luck, and called by to see E.T. Mensah at his pharmacy in Zion Street.

> Fortunately E.T.'s wife, who is from Calabar, knew my father as she used to buy things from his shop. In fact she started to cry and said my dad was a real human being and a beautiful person — always helping people. So she told E.T. he had to take me. So E.T. had to buy me some heavy clothes, for in those days musicians had to wear trousers, white shirt and bow-tie.

Kofi became the youngest member of the Tempos, played bongos for them and was also their 'Gungadin', the old West African term for road manager. He toured the whole of West Africa with this band and fondly remembers the help E.T., or the 'old man' as he affectionately calls him, gave him at the start of his career.

Rhythm in demand

However, time never stands still, and when Kofi was offered a job as conga player by Tommy Gripman he joined the Red Spots dance band in 1961 — for he wanted to progress and they gave him room for solos.

This was a busy time for Kofi, as he was so much in demand that he played with other bands as well, for example, the Gagarin band set up by the Ghana TUC and named after the Russian cosmonaut, Yuri Gagarin. He also teamed up with four Italian musicians belonging to Silvio Cambert's group, which played Latin-American music at cabaret spots in town. They got on so well that, in 1963, the Italians decided to take the band home and on tour, and asked Kofi to choose three more Ghanaian musicians to accompany them. The eight-piece band stayed three months in Italy. Then they drove a Fiat to Yugoslavia, Greece, Turkey and all the way to Baghdad in Syria. In fact they got lost for a time in the Syrian desert on Christmas day but luck was on their side.

> By the grace of God we met one of these camel drivers. They can just look at the sun and tell us exactly which direction to go. So we got to Baghdad and played at the Ali-Baba Club. We were a big success, as Cuban music was popular there.

But trouble arose between the Italian and Ghanaian members over the problem of playing Turkish music. The Italians had even been having trouble with the Highlifes but the Turkish music completely floored them.

> The Turkish music was in 6/8, 9/8 and 12/8 time. The Italians couldn't play it as their syncopations were never there. Then Princess Amina, a Turkish dancer came to join us and after

Kofi with wife and child

twelve days the Italians couldn't play for her. We, the Ghanaians, were playing it within three minutes. This led to friction and the band scattered.

Kofi stayed with Princess Amina for four years and toured the Far East, Europe and West Africa with her, finally parting company in Sweden.

Kofi stayed put in Sweden where he taught music and rhythm at the National Ballet School, and also put together a band, called Modern Sounds, with some West Indian friends. They toured all over Scandinavia. This band used steel drums, congas, trap-drums, piano and guitars and played every kind of music, including classical pieces by Bach, Beethoven and Strauss. Kofi also composed several songs for them, based on the traditional Ewe Agbadza beat. These were played on Swedish television and one song *Otinku* was recorded by EMI in 1969.

Between gigs and teaching, the ever-dynamic Kofi also played with the Swedish Symphony Orchestra as percussionist. He worked with any Jazz musicians who visited the country, like Duke Ellington, Jack McDuff, Miles Davis, Alexis Korner and Sarah Vaughan.

Then in 1973, after a jam-session in Oslo, he was invited to join the Afro-rock band Osibisa whose leaders, Teddy, Mac and Sol, he knew well from Ghana.

> When I joined Osibisa it was the same old travelling business. The first record I made with them was *Superfly TNT*, which was the soundtrack of a film about

a Black American guy going to East Africa. After that we got signed on to Warner Brothers and did *Happy Child* and *Osibirock* for them. Then the band signed up with Bronze in 1975 and we made *Welcome Home*.

Three of Osibisa's successful songs were written by Kofi. These were *Happy Children*, *Somaja* and *Kilele*.

In 1977 Osibisa played at FESTAC in Nigeria, did a big show in Ghana and then went straight on the road yet again, this time to the West Indies. But, as Kofi explains, he was getting tired of all this travelling.

> I met a lovely woman and decided to be a family man and give up the travelling and living out of a suit-case. So I left Osibisa.

One of the first things he did after leaving them was to release a Disco album on the Bronze label with Kiki Gyan, who also left Osibisa at the same time. Then he went into producing records himself. He started by producing a record with the Reggae band called Tradition and then started to help High Tension, a funk band made up of young West Indians living in London whom Kofi knew.

> For when they were young kids they used to come around to see me and sing and I taught them to play drums. Then I got a deal for them on Island Records, as Chris Blackwell is a good friend of mine. I co-produced them with Alex Sadkin, Bob Marley's engineer. Then they hit

the charts. The song *Hi Tension* made it to number thirteen in the British charts, and the follow-up *British Hustle*, made it to number eight.

In 1980 Kofi decided to take a short break from family life and went on a tour of the States and the Caribbean with Jimmy Cliff, and recorded a few tracks with him.

His last project in England, before going off to the Netherlands, was his very first solo album *Kofi* on the CBS label. This was partly recorded at Eddy Grant's Coach House Studios, partly at Island Studios and partly at Phonodisc near Ibadan in Nigeria. This album boasts many top West Indian and West African musicians. Ed Bentley (Ghana), Louis Becket (Antigua) and Kiki Gyan (Ghana) on keyboards, Eddy Grant (Guyana) on traps and guitar, Jimmy Hynes (Barbados) on bass, Jake Solo (Nigeria) on guitar, Papa Mensah (Ghana) on drums, Mike Odumosu (Nigeria) and Tokurboh Shortade (Nigeria) on bass, Keith Mackintosh (West Indies) on moog, Ray Allen (Ghana) sax, Lloys Clark (Jamaica) on sax, Hershall (West Indies) on trumpet, Amoa (Nigeria) on talking drums, and Uwandile (Zimbabwe) and Dora Ifudu (Nigeria) on vocals. Kofi has decided that this first solo album is to be released in Africa before Europe as he feels that, from his new Dutch base, he will be concentrating on the African market, rather than on the English one. In fact he hopes ultimately to get back home and set up his recording company there.

8 Sonny Okosun's Afro-reggae

One of the most successful African sounds is that of Sonny Okosun from the mid-west of Nigeria. For the last ten years Sonny has been pounding out a series of distinctive styles, a blend of the local roots music of the Bendel State and Western Rock and Reggae.

His first sound, which came off the production line in the early seventies, was the 'Ozzidi' beat, in which he combined the Highlife music of his home town of Benin City with a touch of Santana-like guitar. Then, from 1977, he began releasing his Afro-reggae hits and has now turned to his own special type of Disco music. His music is now heard all over Africa, the Caribbean and in the Black communities of Europe and the States. In fact his songs of peace are in such demand, that he was the first Nigerian musician to play in newly independent Zimbabwe, and he is constantly on tour, both at home and abroad.

He works for London-based EMI and is so ambitious that he wants to become one of their directors! Final touches to Sonny's releases are done at the London studio, but the basic tracks are laid down at the EMI studio in Lagos. His engineer there is the dedicated and tireless Emmanuel Odemusi, one of the best sound engineers of West Africa.

Salary: one shirt

But let's start in the eastern Nigerian town of Enugu, where Sonny was brought up and where he was in contact with artists right from the beginning. Both his mother and grandmother were expert singers, dancers and traditional story-tellers. His first intention was to become a Hollywood actor and, as Sonny explains, when he was a teenager he became a Pop fanatic.

6 I was inspired by Elvis Presley and watched his film *Loving You*. And also Cliff Richard's *Expresso Bongo*. I wanted to be a great man like them when I saw how many fans they had. Sometimes I used to sleep at the Rio Cinema in Enugu after watching all the films. 9

But when Sonny left school, it was towards acting that he first turned.

6 When I grew up I joined a drama group as I was so interested in acting. It was called the Eastern Nigerian Theatre and was led by John Okwerri, who started the Mbari Centre in the East. The Mbari Centre was an organisation originally started by a White man to force us to know our roots. It had big offices at Ibadan and Enugu and Nigerian writers like Wole Soyinka and J.P. Clarke were seriously involved. 9

At the Centre all the actors, playwrights and musicians could meet. It was there that Sonny first took an interest in playing guitar. His first guitar was actually bought for him by Mrs Miriam Okagbue, now head of the Imo State Broadcasting and Television station.

At first he began playing just for fun, but then, in 1966, he formed his first group called the Postmen.

6 It was the first Pop group in the eastern region and we played the music of Elvis, Cliff and the Beatles. We never earned anything. The television people used only to pay us with a shirt each, after three months' of weekly performances. 9

When the Nigerian Civil War broke out, Sonny moved to Lagos where he started to work as a graphic designer for television as he wanted to 'get as close to acting and music as possible'.

Then in 1969 he teamed up, as second guitarist, with the Melody Maestros, led by the master of the Benin sound, Sir Victor Uwaifo. Sonny learnt a great deal during the two years he was a member of this band and toured Europe and Japan with them.

Ozzidi

By 1972 Sonny decided it was time to form his own group which he first called Paperback Limited but shortly afterwards changed to Ozzidi. The name Ozzidi is that of a traditional Ijaw god. Here is Sonny's explanation of how the sound was created:

6 I originally wanted to be a playwright and tell the world about Shango, Chaka Zulu and the deep, deep history of Africa. That's why I named my band Ozzidi. I studied Victor Uwaifo's style of composition so, when I left, I thought if I am to be recognised, I

must have my own rhythm. So I combined the African rhythm with the Beatles' style of playing, as I wanted a rhythm that anyone in the world could listen to. I am very proud that they can appreciate my records in America, Britain and even South Africa. **'**

Sonny's first recording success with his Ozzidi music was the single *Help* which sold over 100,000 copies in Nigeria, followed by three albums, *Ozzidi, Living Music* and *Ozzidi for Sale*, which all sold 100,000. This music was heard up and down the West African coast, and Sonny made many tours with his band and two glamorous stage dancers.

Sonny goes reggae

In 1977 Sonny changed to his Reggae sound and, as he explains, it all happened by chance.

' It was almost an accident, as I was recording six tracks for EMI and needed a seventh to fill the record up. That was my Reggae song *Help* which ended up being the biggest hit. It is a simple traditional Bini song but written in English. I got the rhythm from Ogunde the playwright. I do believe the Reggae rhythm came from our side, for when I met Jimmy Cliff in New York, before he came to Nigeria, he actually said he was playing Highlife. And in fact if you listen deeply to Reggae it has a Highlife formation. The only difference is the modified beat. **'**

It was Afro-reggae that really made Sonny a superstar and after

Sonny Okusun

44

the success of *Help*, released on an album and as a single, he made an album specifically featuring his new sound. This was *Papa's Land*, which sold 150,000 copies in Nigeria. EMI was so pleased that, in 1977, they sent Sonny to their Abbey Road studio in London, made famous by a band that Sonny idolises — the Beatles. There he recorded *Fire in Soweto* and *Holy Wars*, two albums that sold over 150,000 copies in Nigeria alone, and became best sellers internationally.

Into Disco

Never one to stand still for a moment, Sonny has recently gone over to a third sound, a Disco version of his earlier Ozzidi music. I asked him what made him decide to do this:

American Disco music has taken over Africa. During the days of Victor Olaiya, the Uhurus, and Ramblers dance bands there was Jazz music from America. Then there was Pop music. It never gave us musicians a chance to move out. And you know with Africans, anything that comes from England is a gas. Then during the time of Victor Uwaifo and Fela there was this Soul music.

I always remember that one day Victor Uwaifo printed some handbills saying that no-one should listen to Soul music. But I think that Soul music is like our Aladura (praying) songs — it's a spiritual music. But they came down and took the business from us.

Now these days we have Funk, but I'm not lying low and I won't let it take gari from my hands.

So I have decided to create my own type of African Disco music. Believe me sincerely, it is catching on like wildfire. This music we hope to export to America and England.

His first Disco song was the track *No More Wars*, which appears on his *Third World* album and is sung in Yoruba. This was followed by an album catering exclusively for this music called *The Gospel According to Ozzidi*, sung in both Yoruba and English. When I saw Sonny in 1981, in London, he was putting the finishing touches to a follow-up to these Disco hits.

Many of Sonny's songs, especially the later ones, have a strong theme of African Liberation and peace and so I asked him what he thought the role of a musician in society should be.

It is a god-given talent, just like a great football player, a boxer like Muhammad Ali, or Bruce Lee. So a musician owes a lot to society, as he sees more. Whatever we see, we store it in our memories and it explodes in the studio or on stage. We are talking to the world. You see, a musician is a lecturer and he can't do anything he likes. He has to wear a good dress or trousers. A musician has to correct society, as he has followers and fans — as I once discovered when there was a rumour that I had died. When I got to Enugu, my friends thought I was a ghost, as did a big crowd of followers.

I sing protest songs and songs of truth. Like my song *We Don't Want to Fight Wars No More*

which was played on radio and television in Nigeria when the Nigeria and Cameroon conflict burst. I don't sing Tom Jones-type songs about love.

Sonny's social awareness is not only expressed in the lyrics of his songs, for he is actively involved in helping set up a Musicians' Industrial Board under the Minister of Culture, to defend artists' rights and replace the fragmented Musicians' Union of Nigeria.

Sonny is involved in setting up yet another union because he wants Nigeria to catch up with Ivory Coast.

When I was in Abidjan I was handled by the Ivory Coast Musicians' Union, a very strong union as you get all your royalties and mechanical rights. It's one of the best music unions in Africa. About 1978 I discussed with my manager about setting up a Musicians' Industrial Board and we went about getting some guys together, like Sunny Ade, Ebeneezer Obey, Victor Uwaifo and musicians from the East. In the near future the government will recognise us, but up to now it hasn't, as our Board will take the cake from the Ministry of Youth, Sport and Culture who haven't been active and know little about the modern Nigerian music scene. We want the Board to be represented by a single Minister of Culture. But when the Industrial Board is recognised it will be stronger than the old Musicians' Unions.

9 Highlife Explosion

Everywhere in West Africa people are dancing to Highlife music, a close cousin of West Indian calypso. If not Highlife, then they're grooving to dance-styles derived from it, like Juju music, Afro-beat and Kpanlogo.

The name, Highlife, was coined about sixty years ago when local African melodies were first orchestrated by brass bands and stylish Black dance orchestras. Later on it was 'jazzed up' by the famous Ghanaian trumpeter E.T. Mensah, the 'King of Highlife' whose Tempos band spread this music around West Africa in the 1950s. But even though Highlife started off in the coastal towns, it soon spread into the rural areas, where it was played on traditional percussion instruments and the acoustic guitar, and went under names like Native Blues, Palm-Wine music, Ashiko music, Makossa music in the Cameroons and Maringa in Sierra Leone. Today, it is this more indigenous form of guitar band Highlife that has burst into the popular music scene.

Highlife in Ghana

But first let us turn to Ghana, the recognised birthplace of Highlife. In Ghana in the sixties, Highlife there was flowing in two streams: dance bands like E.T. Mensah's Tempos, Broadway, Uhurus and the Ramblers playing Highlife with a Jazz and Calypso touch, and the guitar bands playing an electrified Palm-Wine music whose audience was in rural areas and among the city poor.

Since the sixties, the dance bands have more or less folded up, as the youth identify them with 'colo' or colonial and prefer Western Pop music. In fact some of the dance bands, like the Black Beats, have turned into Pop groups.

But this did not happen to the guitar bands, although they did absorb ideas from Pop. In the seventies there was a general expansion of this music, absorbing new ideas, while maintaining and strengthening its traditional roots.

One of the first signs of this development was around 1970, with the amazing success of C.K. Mann and his Carousel Seven. They became all the rage with their 'Osode' music, the roots Highlife of Cape Coast. Their albums on the Essiebons label, such as *Party Time* and *Funky Highlife*, were in such demand that the shops ran out.

Even some of the older generation of guitar band leaders, like E.K. Nyame and Kwaa Mensah, started to re-release, in stereo form, some of their old hit singles from the fifties. E.K. Nyame started to release a series of albums under the title *Sankofa* or 'go back and retrieve', and continued right up to his death in 1977.

Koo Nimo

A fascinating combination of traditional Ashanti Palm-Wine music, classical guitar techniques and Jazz has been created up in Kumasi by Dan Amponsah, or Koo

Nimo as he is known in the music business. I first met him in 1973 after having been knocked out by one of his tapes, that I had heard in 1970, recorded privately by a friend of mine. From the sound of the music I expected to meet an ancient grey-haired Palm-Wine guitarist, but he has the appearance of a youngish, vigorous man, as much at ease playing local Ashanti Blues as modern Jazz. In 1980 he became the President of the Musicians' Union of Ghana (MUSIGA).

Koo Nimo was born in 1934. His father was a guitarist and a trumpeter in the local village brass band. He was given a thorough classical training by German missionaries, at his Presbyterian school in Kumasi. Later, when he took up the guitar seriously, there were two major influences on his style. One was the guitar band leader Onyina, from Kumasi who, in the fifties, began creating a unique blend of Highlife using Jazz chord progressions. Then there was the English pathologist, Professor Laing, who became Koo Nimo's musical godfather and arranged for him to study classical guitar. He went to England to study as a laboratory technician where he was exposed to even more musical styles.

 My Spanish influences are from Carulli, Carcassi, Julian Bream and John Williams (whom I once met). Kurt Anderson, Duke Ellington's first trumpeter, also became a great friend of mine. I met Count Bassie's guitarist, Freddie Green. I met Charlie Bird who influenced me a lot. And I met the prolific composer Jack Duarte who's got a wonderful record library. For guitar, my influences were Django Rheinhardt, Charlie Christian, Wes Montgomery and Jim Hall. Professor Laing also exposed me to Dizzie Gillespie, Thelonius Monk and Miles Davies. I also like the Oriental music I heard in Manchester, especially the thing that was like a calabash (tabla drums). In Manchester I got to know the Indian community as I liked their peppers and used to practise yoga. '

This is how Koo Nimo sees the development of his music:

' I'm going to marry traditional Highlife guitar with Spanish and Latin-American music and Afro-Spanish style, using traditional rhythms and arpeggio. I always use finger picking, never the plectrum. Also I want to develop an Afro-jazz and use Wes Montgomery and Charlie Christian-type chords in it. I'm also thinking of bringing in the European flute and the durugya, which is the Akan horn played when an old chief dies. It has very low tones and is very melancholic. My other interest is drumming and I've got a boy I have adopted, called Little Noah. I picked him up when he was nine and he is revolutionising my band. He plays the talking drums. '

After all that, how can anyone say that Palm-Wine music is old fashioned and on the way out! Koo Nimo is keeping the sound young through constant modification to all its aspects.

Ga street music

A Highlife folk revival has been going on in the south of Ghana in and around Accra, where Ga street music, sea-shanties, Highlifes and Kpanlogos are now becoming popular with young and old. Until the 1970s Ga music had hardly ever been recorded, unlike the Ashanti or Akan Palm-Wine and guitar band music. But since then, a large number of Ga 'cultural groups', as they are called, have emerged, using traditional drums and the acoustic or 'box' guitar. Wulomei was the first band to make this Ga cultural music commercially successful, and many others have followed, like Abladei, Dzadzaloi, Adjo, African Personality, Agbafoi and Suku Troupe. After fifty years, Ga music has finally hit the music scene with a vengeance.

Wulomei

Wulomei is a group formed by the drummer Nii Ashitey and impressario Saka Acquaye in 1973. On stage Wulomei, which, in Ga language, means Fetish priests, dress up in the frilly white caps and white cloth of the traditional Ga medicine priests and priestesses. Nii Ashitey, leader and chief priest of the group, darts in and out of his group, directing them with staccato bursts of rhythm on his long Osraman drum, which he slings over his shoulder. Musicians include the solo guitarist, percussionists, the front line of vocalists and the bamboo flute players. Percussion instruments are local congas, bells, maraccas and the giant Gome or Gombe drum which

plays the bass line. This huge drum played with hands and heel, is played by the biggest member of the band, Nii Adu or 'Big Boy' who sits on top of it, shaking like a jelly.

Wulomei is not only popular with Gas, but has crossed all boundaries in Ghana. At their dances and shows, one finds young and old, rich and poor, Ga and non Ga, all enjoying themselves. Nii Ashitey formed his group, he said 'to bring something out for the youth, to progress and forget foreign music and do their own thing'.

Ashitey started his musical career in the 1940s when, still a small boy, he joined the Navy Babies, one of Accra's many Konkomba groups of the time. Later on he became the conga player for E.T. Mensah's Tempos and then went over to Liberia to join President Tubman's Stars Dance Band. After this he returned home to play for the Ghana Police Band and the Workers' Brigade Band Number Two, before going on to form Wulomei.

He told me that Wulomei incorporates music from many local sources, the most important being Kpanlogo, a fusion of local Ga music and Highlife. In fact when Kpanlogo drumming and dancing was first created in the early sixties by the Ga youth, the elders banned it as they considered it to be indecent. A terrific row blew up between the young and old, so President Nkrumah was called in to give the final verdict. Happily he gave it the go-ahead.

Wulomei's first album, released in 1974, was an instant success. It was called *Walatu Walasa* and was dedicated to the government's self-reliance policy. Then, in 1975, they

Koo Nimo of Ghana

signed a three-year contract with Phonogram and released an album called *Wulomei in Drum Conference*. The same year, they accompanied the Kwaa Mensah Palm-Wine group and the Gonje (one-stringed violin) group of Salisu Mahama of northern Ghana, on a six-week tour of the USA. The group split after that and Naa Amanua formed Suku Troupe.

The African Brothers

The Ghanaian Highlife scene would be incomplete without the African Brothers — top of the league of the hundred and fifty or so electric guitar bands of the country. The leader of the group is Nana Ampadu from the hilly Kwahu region of Ghana, who formed his band in the early

sixties. Their first big success was the record *Ebi Tie Ye* (Some Live Well) released in 1967, which they later made into a play. The theme of the song is the growing division of society into rich and poor. In the traditional African fashion this topic is dealt with in parable form — in this case the bigger animals push the smaller ones away from the warmth of the camp fire.

Since that first hit, Ampadu and his group of musicians and actors have been barn-storming Africa and have made several international tours as well. The band not only has a full rhythm section of trap-drums, congas, maraccas and clips, but even the guitars are used to set up cross-rhythms. The group uses four guitars that set up a scintillating network of sound, boosted by the distinctive touch of Ancient on keyboards.

Ampadu himself is a lightly built man who literally oozes energy. But he does not dominate the stage like a European superstar. Rather he holds back and then suddenly breaks in with a little guitar riff or solo, sending the music of the band to a new and higher level of intensity. Then he retires for a while and comes back again, each time magically raising the vibrations of the players and dancers.

His band doesn't only play top quality Highlifes. Ampadu is always creating new dance beats for his numerous fans: the 'Loco-motive' — a funky Highlife rhythm; Afro-hili — a combination of High-life and Afro-beat; a beautiful blend of Highlife and Reggae called Afro-reggae, to mention a few.

Ampadu's one-time partner was Eddie Donkor, another master of the guitar who has gone on to form his own band. But Ampadu never seems to run out of brilliant musicians. And his latest is Mumbi, a female vocalist, whose wistful, melancholy voice fits in perfectly with the bubbling rhythms of African Brothers.

Besides all the touring and recording, Ampadu has also found time to organise a nationwide society for the guitar bands and

acting groups of Ghana. He is the driving force behind the Ghana Indigenous Musicians' Co-opera-tive (GHACIMS), set up in 1974 to protect and promote the interests of guitar bands.

Highlife in Sierra Leone and the Cameroons

Sierra Leone is another main centre of Highlife development. There are a number of top guitar bands like the Afro-nationals and Sabannah 75, whose music is now selling in Europe. There is an updated form of Maringa Palm-Wine music, called Milo Jazz, that is very popular locally. Similarly, Makossa music, the Cameroonian form of Highlife, is a base for new creations like the Disco Makossa of superstar Manu Dibango. The band, Voory's Power, also from the Cameroons, joined up with the Grenadians dance band of Lagos and fused Makossa with Nigerian Afro-beat.

Highlife in Nigeria

Nigeria is now the major centre for Highlife because it has recor-ding and pressing facilities. In the fifties it was all Highlife dance band music, introduced to the country by the Ghanaian Tempos band of E.T. Mensah and copied by musicians in Lagos, such as Victor Olaiya, Bobby Benson and E.C. Arinze. Guitar band music was around, but very submerged in the commercial music scene.

Then, in the mid-sixties, every-thing changed, because of the Nigerian Civil War. Many of the dance bands, led by Nigerians from the east, collapsed, like those of

Charles Iwegbue, Enyang Hen-shaw, Zeal Onyia, E.C. Arinze and Rex Lawson. The field was left open for the guitar bands, which surfaced as a dominant force. In the western part of Nigeria, this guitar band music was Juju music, in the mid-west it was Bini High-life and in the east it was Igbo Highlife.

Victor Uwaifo's music (an inter-nationalised version of the Highlife music of the Bendel State) is in fact a sophisticated variation on the local 'Native Blues'.

There are many other Highlife musicians from that area — Collings Oke, and the Odoligue Nobles, who worked with the Melody Maestros; the band leader Dandy Oboy; and Mudogo Osegie who was with Victor from 1966 but left in 1971 to form the Muska-teers. They play a Bini music they call 'Bushpower'. Another leading musician who was initiated by the Melody Maestros is Sonny Okosun, whose Ozzidi music is a mixture of Rock, Reggae and Uwaifo-type Highlife rhythms.

Palm-Wine music and guitar bands have always been popular in the eastern part of Nigeria. The hundreds of records produced by E.K. Nyame of Ghana were a formative influence on this style. There were many local groups too, like Okonkwo Adigwe from Asaba and Aderi Olariechi from Owerri. In the fifties and early sixties it was the Highlife dance bands rather than guitar bands that stole all the limelight.

With the Civil War in Nigeria, the dance bands collapsed and then Rex Lawson, leader of the most popular Highlife band, the Rivers-men, was killed in an accident. The

Highlife tradition was kept alive by the guitar bands, Rex Lawson's influence always remaining important. In fact after Lawson's death, the Riversmen formed the Professional Seagulls, a top guitar band right up to the present day. The Peacocks, formed in Owerri in 1970 by Raphael Amanabae, who was a member of the Riversmen, were also influenced by Rex Lawson's music. The Philosophers National, formed by the late Celestine Ukwu is a top guitar band in Nigeria today. Born in 1942, at the age of twenty Celestine joined his first group, Michael Eleagha's Paradise Rhythm Orchestra based in Enugu. Celestine then formed his own group in Onitsha in 1966, called the Music Royals, later to become the Philosophers.

Paulson Kalu and his Africana is a very popular band from Aba. And from Owerri come the Oriental Brothers, who have recently split into two, one wing led by the ace guitarist Dan Satch Opara and the other by the vocalist, Warrior. Both, however, are marketed by the same company, Decca West Africa.

The Soundmakers have been the leading guitar band from the east since 1964. They were formed by Stephen Osita Osadabe. Born in 1936, he joined Stephen Amechi's band in 1959, then went on to form the Central Dance Band before forming the Soundmakers. The popular Ikengas were formed by a breakaway group from this band.

Rokafil Jazz

In the last few years a new sound has been brewing in the east. This is the combination of Highlife with the Congo beat of Zaire, such as the Ogene sound of Oliver de Coque. But most famous of all is Rokafil Jazz which has had a series of smash hits in Africa and the Caribbean since the *Sweet Mother* album, released in 1977. That year in Africa everyone began playing *Sweet Mother*, and African prints, night-clubs, chop-bars and mammy wagons began to bear this name.

The reason for this is clear, as Rokafil Jazz combines all the best from several African countries — the Highlife style of eastern Nigeria, the fast Makossa music of the Cameroons, plus a touch of the guitar style from neighbouring Zaire. In fact the leader of the band, Nicholas Mbarga, or Prince Niko as he is known as on stage, is half Nigerian and half Cameroonian.

The popularity of *Sweet Mother* was also enhanced by the fact that the lyrics were in pidgin English and so could be understood from country to country, while, in addition, Prince Niko's modernised Highlife bass-line, gives a Reggae feel.

Rokafil Jazz followed this hit with more Highlife albums in their fast, bouncy style — *Dear Father*, *Free Education in Nigeria* and *Music Line* are some examples. *Music Line* is literally the story of Nicholas and his band. The song starts with a father warning his son against going into the music business as he will never be able to save enough money to get married and settle down. But it ends happily, with the son becoming so successful through music that he can afford several wives, a big car and is generally extremely rich and powerful.

Prince Niko has become so successful that he has set up his own hotel and club in his home town of Onitsha, where he is preparing to start up a multi-track studio.

Nicholas was interviewed at the BBC's external Broadcasting Centre, Bush House. I was on the same programme, and was astonished to see a diminutive figure breezing in, flanked by a group of heavies, or manager-bodyguards. Unlike his boisterous, noisy companions, Nicholas turned out to be a quiet, almost shy person. He has a lot in common with Nana Ampadu, leader of Ghana's African Brothers band. Both are wiry, slightly-built men with sensitive, fine features. Both are wizard musicians and there is even a resemblance in the Highlife music they play. Although quiet off-stage, in the limelight Nicholas is completely different. On stage Prince Niko looks larger than real life as he wears stacks, or 'guarantee shoes' as they are called in West Africa. After an initial warm-up by the band, he comes on stage dressed like a superstar, wearing bright clothes and a silken cape.

By the end of the two and a half hour show, at a gig I saw in London, he had the audience in the palm of his hand. They were dancing in the aisles and in front of the stage and would have gone on all night if the caretaker hadn't come and closed the place. He did only the one gig in London before flying off to Paris to do a promotion tour. His music is popular everywhere and he is spreading Highlife music far and wide.

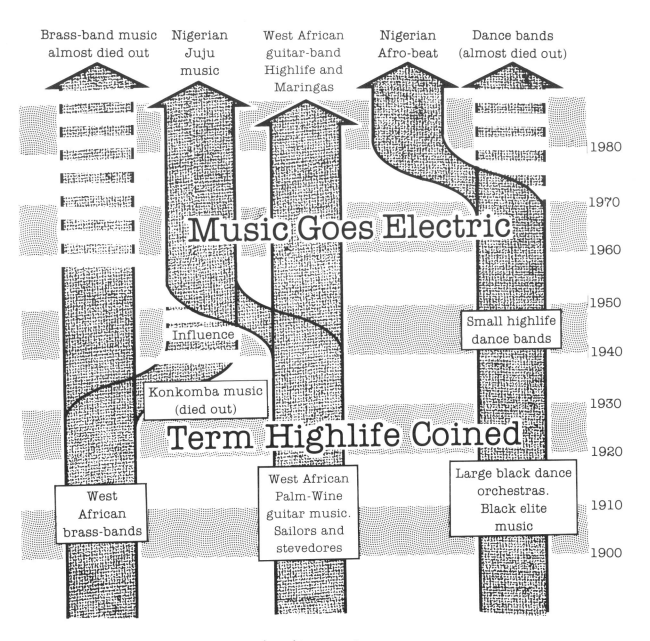

Brass-band music almost died out — Nigerian Juju music — West African guitar-band Highlife and Maringas — Nigerian Afro-beat — Dance bands (almost died out)

Music Goes Electric

1980
1970
1960
1950
1940
1930
1920
1910
1900

Influence

Konkomba music (died out)

Term Highlife Coined

Small highlife dance bands

West African brass-bands

West African Palm-Wine guitar music. Sailors and stevedores

Large black dance orchestras. Black elite music

Highlife Tree (some people say that Highlife is dead, this diagram demolishes this myth and shows how Highlife has evolved)

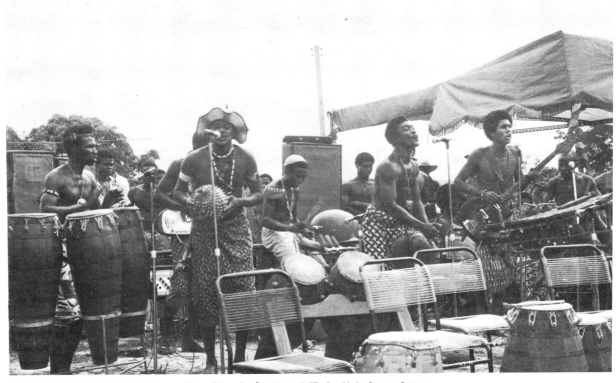

The Afro-fusion band Hedzolleh from Accra

10 'F' Promotions, Ghana's Melting Pot

Faisal Helwani and the Napoleon night-club

One of the main catalysts in the Ghanaian music scene over the last fifteen years or so has been the impressario and producer Faisal Helwani. His Napoleon night-club in Accra has been a central melting pot for musical talent from home and abroad, and from there a stream of top bands has moved into the international field.

Faisal was born in Sekondi in 1946 and has been fascinated by music ever since he launched his 'F' Promotions in 1964 when he began organising student pop competitions or 'Pop Chains'. In 1968 he formed his first group, the El Sombraros led by Alfred Banner-man and Johnny Acheampong and started promoting Fela Aníkúlápo-Kuti in Ghana. Fela's Koola Lobitos and the El Sombraros toured Ghana several times together.

In 1968 Faisal organised his most ambitious promotion to date; a one and a half month tour of East Africa by the Uhurus dance band led by Stan Plange, the Rolling Beats dance troupe and the drummer Kofi Ghanaba (Guy Warren). After this success, he opened up his night-club, first called the Pagadeja and from 1973 on, the Napoleon — Ghana's first discotheque.

His first resident band there was Hedzolleh (Freedom) which combined Rock and African music and won the Ghana Arts Council dance band award in 1974. Hedzolleh was led by Stanley Todd of the El Pollos rock group and a number of musicians from the Arts Council, like Nii Poumah on flutes and Okyerema Asante on percussion. They played Afro-rock more African than Osibisa, and their best hit was *Rekpete*, an old Liberian sea-shanty and Palm-Wine song.

With this band, Faisal was able to spear-head the movement experimenting with new African sounds, and raise its technical level to the sophistication of Disco. Hedzolleh was his first attempt along these lines. The South African trumpeter, Hugh Masekela, was so impressed by Hedzolleh that he worked on an album with the group called *Introducing Hedzolleh with Hugh Masekela*. They were so successful that Hedzolleh ended up touring the USA with Hugh where they released a beautiful album called *The Boys Doin It*.

An Afro-American drummer friend, Jumma Santos, took me for the first time to the Napoleon in 1974. To be honest I was a bit reluctant to go as I didn't like Disco music much at all, after playing with 'bush' guitar bands for some years. But Jumma told me they had a band called the Bunzus that played Highlifes and so I went.

To my ears they were a sensation, as under Faisal's production they had modernised Highlife beautifully. The lead guitarist and leader of the group, Cliff Eck, was using a mellow Rock tone on his guitar, rather than the high-pitched and 'tinny' sound favoured by many local bands. Eddie Agyepong, on traps, had an interesting collection of Western bass-drum, cymbals and high-hat with African cow-bells, up-turned calabashes and local drums.

Faisal was made up like a gilded and sequined cowboy. Sometimes he would rush up on stage, grab some sticks and start beating the talking drums frantically, putting everyone on their toes and generally acting as a tonic.

The Afro-trap drums at the Napoleon night-club

53

I'll never forget the therapeutic effect the Napoleon and Faisal had on an Afro-American jazz pianist called Patti Bown. She was languishing, bored and sick, at the Legon University campus, but I got her out of bed and down to the club. That very night she did an organ solo that ended up with her on her back, and the organ on top of her. She got so high she completely forgot about her illness.

Basa-basa, which means pandemonium, was the sister band of the Bunzus, but in spite of the name it was composed of a bunch of very cool guys, mostly Ewes who specialised in Rock fusions of their local Agbadza beat. There were the Nyarko twins, now based in Lagos, on percussion and Abollo the young master-drummer. The leader, Wallace, was the lead guitarist and floated above everyone on stacks. The bassist was beatle-browed Ashela, the hardest working man in show-business. Vocals were supplied by the charismatic Nii Ayitey II whom Faisal was building up into a star, but who later managed to slip out of his grasp to Germany.

It was the Bunzus that particularly attracted me at first and that night with Jumma, I asked Faisal for a jam-session with them. This jam immediately produced two Afro-beat creations we called *Onukpa Shwarpo* and *Yea Yea Ku Yea* which were released by Decca on the *Al Haji Tanko* album and later under the titles *Makola Special* and *Volta Suite* by Makossa of New York.

I played at the Napoleon for two years and during this time performed just about everywhere. We played at the Castle for the Head of State one Sunday, and the following week at a prison! The enterprising Faisal launched a series of shows for prisoners, the first time such a thing had been done in Ghana. We all had to be searched as we entered Ussher Fort in Accra, for matches, cigarettes and so on. When we played, the four hundred male prisoners had to dance 'bone to bone' not 'flesh to bone' (woman to man). One of them got so carried away that he wanted to jam on congas and Faisal agreed. Several years of bottled-up musical frustration burst out of this prisoner who soloed for over half an hour. Faisal promised him a job when he came out, and later on this actually happened.

Faisal also took us out of the country several times, to Togo, Nigeria and the Republic of Benin. We played at Cotonou, the capital of Benin, on the very day of the Marxist revolution and we noticed that everyone seemed to be carrying or waving green branches. In Nigeria we played several times at Fela's Africa Shrine and Victor Olaiya's Papingo night-club.

Whenever we played, the Napoleon's mascot came along. This was the midget Tawia Brown who was a dwarf pimp or 'pilot boy'. Although he was deaf and dumb he always sported miniature copies of the latest fashion including ultra-high guarantee shoes. Occasionally when the spirit took him he would jump up on stage and do a James Brown turn, making odd noises into the microphone, but always on time, as he could 'hear' the beat in his guts.

However, it was the Napoleon that was home-base, and was the place in town where all the musicians, hustlers, pimps and 'good-time girls' hung around until five or six in the morning. It is a maze-like building, built by an eccentric Ghanaian doctor. It has a zoo, aquarium, fountains and many quiet hidden corners that the musicians sussed out. The noisiest place, of course, was the main-gate, watched over by a succession of doormen, hired for their unpleasantness and lack of charm. Security was of prime importance, as the Napoleon, like the Kalakuta in Lagos, was sometimes the target of sabotage attempts. The vibes in the Napoleon were similar to those of the Kalakuta Republic and there was much to-ing and fro-ing between these two fraternal establishments.

Faisal's recording deal with West Africa

In 1977, by which time I had formed my own band, Faisal asked me to contact some of the guitar bands, as he knew I was a member of the guitar band co-operative, GHACIMS. I contacted two of Ghana's grand old men of Highlife music, Kwaa Mensah, nephew of the country's first guitarist, and E.K. Nyame who combined music with acting. I also contacted a cultural group from Labadi called Abladei with whom I had played on a television programme, and a little later the Afro-Spanish guitarist from Kumasi called Koo Nimo.

The day I took E.K. Nyame to the Napoleon, we bumped into Fela just as we were about to leave. I remembered Fela had once told me the high regard he had for E.K.'s pioneering work of the fifties, so when I told Fela he was standing next to E.K., he got really excited, blessed the old musician and invited us the next day to a party at Napoleon.

The guitar bands were to form part of a massive ten-band promotions and recording deal worked out between Faisal and Decca West Africa in Nigeria. Besides Faisal's original groups and those I brought in, there were also the Uhurus dance band, E.T. Mensah's Tempos, Bokoor, the Voices of East Labadi and another cultural group called Adjo. E.K. in the end never signed up as he was already under contract.

These groups played at the Tip Toe Gardens in Accra, which became the main musical venue for a while. During this time the Napoleon was given over to a series of successful Jazz sessions. The bands finally ended up in Lagos at the Decca studios. Particularly successful was an album of 1950s hits by E.T. Mensah called *The King of Highlife*. Faisal became so inundated with musical material that he had to launch his own radio programme and finally set up his own multi-track studio in the Napoleon itself.

From 1974 onwards, the Napoleon not only became the main musical centre of Accra, but also became the headquarters for the Musicians' Union of Ghana (MUSIGA), until it moved premises in 1980 to the Community Centre on the Accra High Street. For many years Faisal financed the union and fought to re-vitalise this moribund organisation. In 1979 he succeeded in creating a radical interim executive which organised

Edikanfo

the great march for recognition the same year. Faisal's latest MUSIGA project is to finance a union newspaper.

From 1979, his preoccupation with music politics didn't leave Faisal much time, so his bands were rather neglected for a while, although many of the tapes were processed and pressed. But once the union was firmly established he was able to turn his full attention again to music. This is when he opened up his own studio and launched a new band called Edikanfo, a large dance ensemble that concentrates on local melodies with a funky touch.

Stars visit the Napoleon

Many stars have recently visited the Napoleon. First there was New Wave's Brian Eno, who flew in from New York and stayed at the Napoleon as Faisal's guest for three weeks. Brian worked with Edikanfo in Faisal's studio and released an album of them on his E.G. record label.

Then a few months later in 1981, Mick Fleetwood, George Hawkins and Todd Sharpe came down to Ghana for a six-week safari, complete with recording engineers, bodyguards and twelve tons of equipment, including a 16 track studio. Mick Fleetwood is the English leader and drummer of Los Angeles-based rock group, Fleetwood Mac. They were expecting to trek around in the bush, and even brought mosquito nets and portable latrines with them. Instead everything was laid on for them by MUSIGA and Faisal, and they were put up at the Star Hotel in Accra. Instead of chasing the musicians the musicians came to them, and they were able to spend their whole time recording on the equipment they set up at the Ghana Film studios. An album was later released by them called *The Visitor* which featured the three musicians plus groups from Ghana like the Super Brains, Koo Nimo's and a children's group. George Harrison of the Beatles played on one track — a dedication to John Lennon.

11 Life on the Road: Modern African Minstrels, The Jaguar Jokers

Drama in Africa is associated with music, dance and works of art. Together they form a holistic art crucial to society, both cementing it together, lampooning it, and accommodating social change, through this fusion of creative energy and social process. For example, there are the traditional roving minstrels and troubadors of West Africa, who are historians, praise singers and entertainers. Then there are the masquerades found throughout the continent and even taken to the New World, such as the masked Jamaican carnival and the mardi gras. The Ashantis of Ghana also have their dramatised Ananse (the spider stories) — satirical morality tales that have found their way to North America as Nancy stories, and to Surinam, through the diaspora. African theatre was, and is, performed out of doors. A raised platform separating audience and performers was never used, not even in traditional theatres, such as the travelling Apidan troupes of the Yorubas. The stage was brought in by the Europeans through the introduction of Cantata or Bible plays, and schoolboy plays performed during Empire day celebrations.

A third influence on African drama was Black Minstrelsy introduced from America around the turn of the century by visiting Vaudeville artists, Ragtime performers, and later by silent movies such as those starring Al Jolson.

It was in Ghana where the fusion

Baba John Bull on a cover of a Nigerian comic

of traditional and modern acting first crystallised in the 1920s in what was known as the concert party. By the fifties there were similar travelling theatres all over Africa. Miriam Makeba worked with one for a time in South Africa. Then in Nigeria there was Hurbert Ogunde's theatre. He was the father of modern Nigerian theatre. In Ghana there was the Akan Trio of E.K. Nyame which combined acting with Highlife music.

In those times many of the plays had a nationalistic flavour. One of Ogunde's plays, *Strike the Hunger* was even banned by the British in 1945. Ghanian Concert Parties were staging plays like *Nkrumah is a Mighty Man* and *Nkrumah Will Never Die.*

Today there are thousands of these popular theatres around Africa. In Lagos State alone there are over two hundred travelling theatres, such as those of Baba John Bull, Baba Mero, Oje Lapido, Moses Olaiya and Kela Ogunmola. All of them stage plays in Yoruba and Hausa to the accompaniment of local music and dance. These days many of the acting groups bring out their most popular plays in comic form.

In East Africa, too, travelling theatres abound and governments there take them very seriously. They are especially encouraged in socialist countries like Tanzania and Mozambique because these plays develop political awareness and educate people.

Concert parties in Ghana

In Ghana there are several hundred Concert Parties/Highlife groups at present and they have

Mr Bampoe, leader of the JJs

even formed their own co-operative. The Jaguar Jokers, a Ghanaian Concert Party, was formed by Mr Bampoe in 1954 and has been on the road ever since. This means that the JJs must surely be one of the hardest-working groups in show-business. They've been on the road for almost thirty years, perform fifteen to twenty shows a month, with each show lasting over six hours. In fact the first time I joined them, as guitarist, for a three-week trek I lost half a stone in weight!

The group makes twelve treks a year touring the towns and villages of Ghana, always starting at the end of the month, pay day, when people have money in their pockets. They send their 'pioneer man' ahead of them. He books the gigs, puts adverts in the papers and sticks posters all over the place.

When the band hits a village, the twenty actors and musicians unload the minibus and set up the equipment (including a portable generator for places without electricity). There are usually no cinemas and clubs in the smaller venues, so usually one of the compound houses in a village or hamlet has a raised stage in its courtyard. If not, the performers have to put up a make-shift stage for the night made from wooden boards and concrete blocks.

Some of the musicians are released from this work as they have to go out in the bus to make 'campaign', with a speaker on the roof of the bus and paintings of scenes from the night's show slung on the sides. Whenever I was with them they used to feature me on these campaigns as a crowd puller,

Baba John Bull standing by his lorry

playing fast Congo Jazz guitar with the conga player. Hordes of children would follow us around as we drove slowly through the dusty streets, thus giving extra publicity. Everyone in sight would stop what they were doing and start to dance. Women with buckets on their heads and children on their backs would start to sway. Old people would get up from their chairs and do a turn to our music. When we returned, everything would be set up for the night's show and the large paintings, or 'cartoons' as they are called, were put outside the theatre to pull in the crowd.

Once, while passing through Swedru in southern Ghana, I had the good fortune to meet the artist who does these paintings for the JJs, and for many of the concert parties. He is called Mark Anthony and he started out as a bar artist, painting murals of 'Highlife' to attract customers. Later on he

began to do pictures for the Spiritual churches and concert parties and now makes his business from this. He is in such demand, that he has to rattle off a twenty square foot painting in just a couple of days.

The JJ's shows start up at about eight in the evening with the band starting to play the *Inside Rhythm*, and the first people beginning to trickle in. Nobody ever comes in before they hear something going on inside. They just hang around the gate until they hear the first few notes of music. This warming-up music includes a selection of all the current popular music, like Highlifes, Souls, Reggaes, Afrobeats, Congo numbers, Pachangas and Smoochie numbers. We would only stop playing when the place was full up. Then the musicians who accompany the actors would play a few of the JJ's best-loved compositions. Anytime between ten and eleven, the play itself starts. First there is an 'opening chorus' when Mr Bampoe, supported by Mr Hammond and the lady impersonator Mr Baidoo, sing and dance Ragtimes and Foxtrots, just as happened at the Ghanaian Concert Parties in the 1920s and 1930s. The dame, Mr Baidoo, wears drag with an expensive wig and spectacles and sings in a falsetto voice.

There are no women in the JJs. All female parts in the acting and singing are performed by men. This is typical of most Ghanaian Concert Parties, although these days a few of the concerts employ women, and a few are led by women. But generally the public has looked down on concert people, making it particularly difficult for women to break into this profession.

After the 'opening chorus', the three principal actors retire to the changing room or 'ante-room', and during this time the audience is entertained by a comic minstrel or 'Bob' as he is referred to in Ghana, usually complete with black and white make-up.

Then, by midnight at the latest, the three-hour play is under way. The JJs have dozens of plays, but normally they stick to one play on any single trek. There are involved stories about orphans and wicked step-parents, the problems of having too many wives, money problems and the clash between the new and old. The very first play the JJs ever performed was about a latrine worker who wasn't being paid for his onerous duties of collecting the night-soil from a certain house. So he went on strike and started throwing excrement from a bucket at his debtors — on stage he used mud!

Mr Bampoe really gets incensed when people claim that concert plays are a corrupting influence, as he considers that, in spite of the slap-stick, they are educative and uplifting. The derogratory attitude to concert parties is slowly beginning to change. Even the government has woken up to the social importance of local comic opera, for in 1973 they initiated the First National Festival of Concert Parties.

Mr Bampoe started acting when he was eleven years old and formed the JJs when he was only twenty. Off-stage he is the quietest of individuals, but in the limelight he literally gets possessed by his bouncy and energetic stage character 'Opia'. Opia is usually a servant in the play — a greedy

Kwaa Mensah's concert party from Ghana in the 1950s

and mischievous imp whom the audience love to hate, but who always ends up helping the hero and heroine of the plot. The character of 'Opia' is in fact an updated version of Ananse the spider; just as is the 'Bob' character, who is a fusion of an American minstrel with Ananse. The difference between them is that the 'Bob' character wears the make-up of a black and white minstrel, whereas Opia only puts on dark pancake. Bampoe originally used to make up like a minstrel, when performing as Opia, but he realised later on that he was copying a White copying a Black. So he cut out the white around the eyes and lips altogether.

All sorts of other characters crop up in the plays. Good-time girls played by the more slender actors, Hausa corporals, bush farmers and town slicks, lawyers, teachers, masked ghosts, evils and angels. The lanky Mr Hammond always plays Mr Johnson and with his deep and sonorous voice is the sermoniser who gives the poetic moral at the end of the night's tale.

Throughout the play the actors keep bursting into song and all movements are accompanied by a guitarist, trap-drummer, hand drummer and clip player who play everything from Pop and Highlifes to Christian hymns and fetish music.

Even though no scenery is used the crowd really gets into the story and joins in by singing, clapping and commenting loudly. I've often seen people weeping and if they really dig an actor or musician they will dance up to the stage and 'spray' or stick money on the performer's forehead. Sometimes it is the other way around as Opia jumps into the crowd, chasing or being chased by someone or something.

The fact that concert parties involve the audience to such a degree and combine music, acting, dance, poetry and painting, illustrates the African attitude to art. From the nineteenth century in Europe there was a marked tendency to fragment the arts into separate categories such as entertainment, music, drama, graphic arts and ballet and make a sharp distinction between audience and performers. The Concert Parties simply combine these different facets of Western art, creating something more in tune with the traditionally integrated art forms of Africa.

The plays are performed in the local languages and are unscripted and so a show can be lengthened or shortened at will, depending on the size and response of the crowd. There is a great deal of improvisation and the actors are such professionals that they cat-nap in the ante-room and have the uncanny ability to wake up at exactly the right moment they are needed on stage. Afterwards they go back to the changing room and fall straight back to sleep again!

The play usually finishes by three o'clock in the morning with the musicians, who started up the evening's show, playing dance tunes again for an hour. The audience really gets their money's worth! Afterwards the performers just crash out on the floor on their mats. Then up by six in the morning to iron and pack, and they are back on the road for the next day's show.

One of the JJ's cartoons

Sometimes, of course, things do not go so smoothly. Once, for instance, at a mining town, the executive of the JJs had a dispute with the locals over the entrance fee — and so refused to play. People were pouring in from the neighbouring villages and getting angry. So we locked ourselves behind the high walls of the theatre to take cover from a hail of stones. Later, when everything had quietened down, we drove off and had two punctures one after the other. Some bright spark had driven nails into our tyres and we had to spend the night stranded in the forest.

These days the JJs are going further afield to the Ivory Coast and Liberia in order to obtain precious foreign exchange needed for repairs and new equipment. One would think that after almost thirty years, the now immensely popular JJs would also be bringing in money from record royalties. But this is not so, as many years ago Mr Bampoe decided never to record. The reason for this was that a close friend of his, who was a well-known concert musician, died under suspicious circumstances. It was claimed that he was poisoned by jealous colleagues who played his record and took the gramophone needles to a fetish priest to cast a spell on them. According to eye-witnesses three needles were found in the dead man's throat.

This happened over twenty years ago and all the time I've known Mr Bampoe I've tried to persuade him to change his mind and start to record, so that he will begin to collect royalties when he has retired from active show business. The problems of transport and the high cost of equipment are so serious in the country that he is now taking this advice. He came to visit me recently and has agreed to record on some recording equipment I have (Bokoor Productions). So his music will go straight onto a pre-recorded cassette and so there will be no problem with poisoned needles!

In September 1982 tragedy struck the JJs when their lorry was involved in an accident in the Aburi Hills. Mr Baidoo was killed, as were the guitarist Kwadwo Doku and percussionist Kwadwo Amankwah. Both Mr Bampoe and Hammond were injured — but they have since decided to put the band together and go back on the road again.

Orchestra Super Mazembe

12 The African-French Connection

French-speaking Africa before Congo music

Before the surfacing of Congo music in the fifties, the French-speaking countries had no modern African dance music. There was plenty of traditional music of course, and imported French music, but the two never met and influenced each other, as the French colonial policy was to keep the indigenous and French cultures quite separate. This is the exact opposite to the British attitude, which encouraged a more flexible approach to the mixing of cultures. This is probably why Highlife and Juju music appeared so much earlier than Congo music, which only exploded onto the African continent in the sixties.

E.T. Mensah, the famous Ghanaian 'King of Highlife', toured French-speaking West Africa in the fifties, before this explosion, and has some interesting views on the difference between the English and French-speaking countries of West Africa.

In the Ivory Coast they were importing European musicians and actors. We saw more of the Whites than the Blacks, as the Whites could afford the night-club life. The White bands were playing Boleros, Cha Cha Chas, Tangos and French music. When we played Highlifes only a few of the Ghanaians there got up and danced. When we were there I never saw an African dance band. **,**

In Guinea Bissau there was a similar situation to this, even in the late fifties. E.T. Mensah and his Tempos visited that country in 1958, just after the Guineans had said, 'No' to De Gaulle's referendum and had opted for complete independence from France. In spite of the peeved French authorities leaving abruptly, and disrupting everything as they went, French musicians stayed on! E.T. remembers seeing them in Conakry: White trios made up of a pianist, violinist and drummer who played French music, Sambas, Rumbas and Boleros. E.T. comments:

' The French dominated the Blacks socially and this affected the music. They had White musicians from Paris, but the African dance music was small. The developments socially and musically in the French territories have occurred since independence and now they want to catch up. **,**

Ignace de Souza, who joined Alfa Jazz, the Republic of Benin's first African dance band in 1953, says the same thing.

' By then, you know, it was the French who were ruling the country and they didn't encourage any dance band music, only the military orchestras. E.T. Mensah

and others used to play as we had some night-club owners who went to Ghana to bring them. **,**

Congo – the fusion of French and African music

It was in the Congo, now called Zaire, that the first successful fusion of French and African music was created. It all started in the early 1950s when Afro-Cuban and Latin-American music, like the Rumba, became incredibly popular in the then Belgian Congo, and was incorporated into the local music. It was played on acoustic guitars, drums and sung in French, Swahili and Lingala. When everything went electric in the sixties the two big names of 'Congo jazz', as the music was called, were Doctor Franco, leader of OK Jazz, and Kallé, leader of African Jazz.

The line-up of Congo Jazz bands is guitars, trap-drums, Afro-Cuban percussion and a front-line of saxophones. The guitarists do not play lead and rhythm, as in the case of Western pop bands. Rather, four or five guitarists playing alto, tenor and soprano, weave in and out of each others' melodies and rhythms creating an intricate pattern of sound. Because of the Rumba influence, this music is quite distinct from that of the former British colonies.

The Zaireans compose cooler dance rhythms than those of Highlife and Jive, and in Congo music there is usually a subtle beginning to the song, which suddenly stops and is followed by an exciting transition leading to the main dance rhythm.

Doctor Franco

Doctor Franco, who is now known as Luambo Makiadi, had managed to keep his band going right up to the present day, although a number of his musicians have split away to form their own groups—for example, his one-time saxist Vercky, who formed the Orchestra Vévé.

Today, OK Jazz is still pumping out albums and Doctor Franco has become so wealthy that he owns three skyscrapers in Kinshasha and half the recording industry there as well!

Kallé's demise and the rise of Tabu Ley

Kallé's band really finished when his two top musicians left to start up their own groups! Doctor Nico, who before joining Kallé had been a technical college teacher, formed his Orchestra African Fiesta in 1966; the vocalist Rochereau left Kallé two years later, and with Guvana and Faugus, two wizard guitarists from the Diamond Blue Band, set up the Orchestra African Fiesta National. Then after several internal changes Rochereau formed the Orchestra Africa in 1972.

It was that year, during the Zairean indigenisation programme, that he changed his name to Tabu Ley. By this time he was the most well-known vocalist in Zaire and had sold over five million records.

Tabu Ley was born in 1940 about a hundred and fifty miles from Leopoldville. He learnt to sing during hunting forays.

The spread of Congo music

Today, there are over five thousand bands in Zaire, and Congo music has spilled out all over Africa.

In South Africa the Zairean style of guitar playing has influenced some of the township bands like the Zulu group, Mshikishi Namagugu. Congo Jazz is also extremely popular in East Africa and many of the contemporary sounds there are based on it. Typical are Gabriel Omollo and his Apollo Komesha, the Les Kinois, the Shirati Jazz band and Super Mazembe from Kenya; and Salim Abdullah's Cuban Marimba Band Super Makassy, Orchestra Kamanyola and Orchestra Safari Sounds from Tanzania.

In Ghana one of the first Congo-type bands to become resident in 1966 was the Black Santiagos led by Ignace de Souza.

Today, one of the top guitar bands that operates in Ghana and Ivory Coast is Francis Kenya's Riches Big Sound, which plays music in the same mould as that of Zaire, but sung in the local Nzima language.

Congo music has also had a big impact on Nigeria, especially in the eastern part of the country, which is closer to Zaire than the rest of the country, and to French-speaking neighbours like Cameroons and Gabon. In the last few years there has been a commercially successful synthesis of Nigerian Highlife with Congo music by bands like Rokafil Jazz and Oliver de Coque's.

Today, in French-speaking Africa there is a musical ferment

M'Pongo Love, a top vocalist from Zaire

63

Mzee Makassy, leader of the Tanzanian band Orchestra Super Makassy

going on, and although musicians started producing their own dance band music later than Nigeria, Ghana, Sierra Leone and Zaire, they are now busily catching up.

Togo

Some of the top bands in Togo are the old-established Melo Togos and newer groups like Eryko Jazz, Orchestra Abass and La Voix d'Agou. Bella Bellow was a very famous pop singer from Togo. From the late sixties until her untimely death in 1973, she recorded many Highlifes, Congo numbers and traditional songs in the local Ewe language. Her most famous release was *Rockia*, a Ewe Pop song, and she was well on the way to becoming West Africa's Miriam Makeba.

Benin

In the neighbouring country of Benin there is the Orchestra Poly-rhythmic de Cotonu playing Zaire-type music and Afro-beats.

Then there is Elrigo and his Los Commandos, Gnonnas Pedro and his Dadjes dance band, which has released a number of albums under the Lagos-based, Take Your Choice label, and Ignace de Souza's Black Santiagos now resident in Lagos.

Ivory Coast

In the Ivory Coast during the sixties, the top band playing the Zaire Sound was the Francois Lougah Orchestra, but today this band also plays Afro-beats. Amedée Pierre and Ernesto Dje Dje are the main exponents of local Highlifes sung in the Dida and Bete languages. Dje's music is the more modern and sounds a bit like the Meringue style played by bands in Sierra Leone like the Afro Nationals. Even more Westernised is Aka Jermome's music which he usually sings in French. The top female vocalist in the country is Aïcha Koje.

Upper Volta

Moving northwards to Upper Volta, the most famous artist is

Ouedraogo, who is backed by a modern instrumental line-up but who sings all his songs in the local Mossi language.

Gabon and the Cameroons

A Gabon artist who has recently released a string of beautiful albums sung in French is the blind guitarist Pierre Akendengue whose group plays a modernised Griot music. Like the traditional Griot music of Africa, Akendengue's lyrics have a strong political and social bias.

He was a student at the Sorbonne and became such an outspoken critic of his government that he had to leave Gabon for a time, until called back to represent his country at FESTAC. His lyrics are present-day parables based on mythological figures like Oreyi, a bloodthirsty monster whom Akendengue equates with a modern Head of State in the pay of imperialism. He gets up to tricks like calling a peace meeting of all the animals and then creating confusion among them so that they devour each other. And there is Marange, the traditional diviner who tries to overthrow the dictator Oreyi.

Cameroons is a neighbour of Gabon and these two countries are tucked between the giants Nigeria and Zaire. Cameroons really gets the best of both musical worlds as it is half English and half French-speaking. The English-speaking part opted to join Nigeria, so the Cameroons has its own version of Highlife called 'Makossa music', which is a very fast and bouncy guitar band style. Congo music is

Jimmy Kutumba, leader of the Ebonies, influenced by the music of Zaire

also popular there, and it is through the Cameroons that Zairean music has influenced the guitar bands of eastern Nigeria. Nicholas Mbarga, the leader of Rokafil Jazz, is half Nigerian and half Cameroonian.

The best-known artist from Cameroons is undoubtedly Manu Dibango. He has been an international star ever since his Disco hit of the early seventies *Soul Makossa* which got into the charts in the USA. Dibango, who plays saxophone, was brought up musically on Makossa music, but today his interests range far and wide. He is adept at Congo music and is also a first rate Jazz and Rhythm and Blues player. For many years he was based in Paris, played at the famous Olympia there, and worked with many top musicians. For instance, he teamed up with the Ivorian musician Francois Lougah with whom he released many albums of Congo and Makossa music. He also worked with the late, great Bella Bellow of Togo. Since his smash-hit *Soul Makossa*, he has released a number of albums combining local African dance music with Jazz and Rhythm and Blues, and he has developed a big following, both at home and abroad. He is currently based in Abidjan where he is the head of the music section and the orchestra of the national radio of the Ivory Coast.

So there's plenty happening in French-speaking Africa today. If things go on like this, maybe this special African fusion music they are creating will come to dominate the French pop scene in France itself!

13 South Africa in Exile: Pushed Out by Apartheid

The South African music scene is quite different from that of the rest of Africa. First of all, the local Black music (Township Jazz and Kwela) was well-known internationally, compared to Highlife, Congo Jazz and Juju music. During the fifties and sixties while the rest of Africa was gaining independence, the apartheid system was set up in South Africa, nipping the development of local music in the bud and pushing its best players into exile abroad.

Before the sixties there was a rich musical heritage in the South African towns stretching back to the turn of this century when Afro-American music first hit the country and when Africa's first recording industry was set up. By the forties and fifties African jazz and variety shows were even becoming popular with Whites — like the music of Miriam Makeba, Dolly Rathebe, Dollar Brand and the Manhattan Brothers.

Then came apartheid and everything was put under government control, including the radio and recording industry. Apartheid also meant the systematic enforcement of segregation and the creation of Black townships like Soweto. All this had a devastating effect on South Africa's jazzmen who lost the venues they had been playing at since the twenties. Alto-saxist Kippie Moeketsi, hailed as South Africa's Charlie Parker, gave up playing altogether for many years. Imported Rock and Roll filled the musical vacuum for the youth of the newly created Black townships.

Many of the Black music stars just upped and left the country like the pianist, Dollar Brand, or Abdullah Ibrahim, as he is now known, who settled in the United States in 1960 with the help of Duke Ellington. Miriam Makeba and Letta Mbulu also went abroad. They both had to switch from Township music, for which they were famous at home, to their own local Zulu and Xhosa folk songs, for which they have become famous internationally. A whole succession of talented South African musicians left, such as trumpeter Hugh Masekela who went to the States and Dudu Pukwana who went to England.

How it all started

Let's first look at the origins of the modern South African music scene and then at the stars in exile.

It began in 1907 when the record market first opened up and Ragtime became a big craze in the African quarters of the towns and cities. In the illegal drinking bars, or shebeens, a local version of Ragtime was soon being churned out on barrel organs and rattles — Marabi music. One of the most popular of the bands playing this music was the Japanese Express. Amongst the wealthier Blacks, Ragtimes sung by refined choirs at evening soirées became the vogue. The most famous of these was conducted by Reuben Caluzza who composed Ragtimes in Zulu and went on to record one hundred and fifty songs for HMV by 1930.

Black American Minstrelsy was also popular during the 1920s and many Black Vaudeville groups and Concert Parties were set up in South Africa — like the Dark Town Strutters, Hivers Hivers and Africans Own Entertainers who tap-danced, sang Ragtimes and Spirituals and performed comic sketches.

Then in the thirties came Jazz and Swing, and the music of Louis Armstrong and Duke Ellington began to influence local bands. The Jazz Maniacs and the Merry Blackbirds began to create the distinctive South African township Jazz. When the kids on the streets began to play local Jazz, they created a poor man's version of it on penny whistles — and called it Kwela. Later, in 1954, a penny whistle tune, *Tom Harke*, by Aaron Lerole, became an international hit.

Popular in the towns, from the thirties on, were variety troupes like the Inkspots and Lucky Stars, which staged plays and played every sort of music from traditional African dances to Township Jazz. The most famous were the Manhattan Brothers who sang Zulu and Xhosa versions of American close harmony music and made so much money for Galo Africa, that this record company employed the first Black talent scout in 1938, Griffiths Motsieloa. These Black variety shows even became popular with Whites, for example the Pitch Black Follies set up in 1937, and then later the variety show *Zonk*, popular with Black and White troops during the Second World War.

King Kong is a more recent example which starred Miriam Makeba and the Manhattan

Louis Moholo

Brothers and opened in Johannesburg in 1959. It was so successful that it was taken to London in 1960. As by then conditions were getting intolerable for musicians back home, half the musicians stayed abroad. This exodus of musical talent has been the picture right up to the present, so let us take a closer look at some of the South African stars who have become musicians in exile.

Miriam Makeba

First there is Miriam Makeba, Africa's number one female vocalist. Her story is a classic one of rags to riches. She was brought up in Johannesburg where her mother was a servant. Miriam loved singing, joining her school choir and also sang at funerals and weddings, both in English and her native Xhosa, a language full of complicated click sounds.

Her first band was the Cuban Brothers, and then, at the seventeen, she joined the eleven-strong Black Manhattan Brothers, the close harmony group modelled on Afro-American bands like the Mills Brothers. Miriam joined them in the mid-fifties and stayed with them for three years, during which time she travelled all over Zaire, Zimbabwe, Zambia and South Africa in a dilapidated bus that kept breaking down.

After she left this hard-working group, she got the lead part in the Black opera *King Kong*, based on the true story of a boxer who kills his lover. In 1960, after the London tour of this show, she stayed on and went on to New York. There Harry Belafonte helped her get her first recording contract in the

States. Here her musical repertoire enlarged to include Calypsos and ballads as well as Jazz and South African Folk songs, and she got her own female harmony group together, the Skylarks or Sunbeams.

Since then she has released many records, like her famous *Phatha-Phatha* and *Malaika* and has made many international tours. Miriam never sings in Afrikaans and has never returned to South Africa, as she is an outspoken opponent of the apartheid system. Some of her songs criticise the repression there and she says she will only return home when her country is independent.

However, she often visits and tours independent Africa, and sang at FESTAC in Nigeria in 1977 and more recently at the packed El Wak stadium in Accra, Ghana, backed by local musicians such as the Todd brothers. Her voice is as powerful as ever. Her daughter, Bongi Makeba is now following in her mother's footsteps, and is based in Paris.

Dudu Pukwana

Many of South Africa's jazz musicians have worked with Dudu Pukwana, and Dudu is a key figure amongst them. He was born and brought up in Port Elizabeth, and was taught his first instrument, the piano, by his father when he was ten years old. In the late fifties he joined his first jazz band called Tete Mbambisa's Four Yanks, based in Capetown. After this, he formed his own band the Jazz Giants which won a jazz award in South Africa in 1963. In that year, he changed over to saxophone and joined the Blue Notes, a Jazz band

Miriam Makeba

▲ Dudu Pukwana and South African singer Pinise Saul of Zila

Otingo, one of the latest South African musicals to hit the West ▼

with some of South Africa's leading musical names — the White pianist Chris McGregor, drummer Louis Moholo, cornet player Mongeza Feza, bassist Johnny Dyani and the late Nick Moyake. They played at the Antibes Jazz Festival in 1964. As the band was multi-racial they had to leave South Africa for good that year. They first went to France and Switzerland and finally settled in England, where they received help from the English Jazz musician Ronnie Scott. They were based in London as the Brotherhood of Breath until 1973, when Chris McGregor left for the South of France.

During the late sixties and early seventies, Dudu Pukuwana and Mongeza Feza, until his untimely death in 1975, asked many of the Blue Notes or Brotherhood of Breath musicians to work with their own groups Spear and Assegai. Dudu worked with many other musicians during this time. He made an album with Hugh Masekela in 1972 called *Home is Where the Music is*, and worked with the American-based South African trombonist Jonas Gwangwa, who was Miriam Makeba's music arranger.

Some of the many musicians who passed through Spear and Assegai were the Nigerian guitarist Fred Coker, bassist Chad Cheido, Ghanaian conga player Terrie Quaye, sax player Bizo Mnqikana and Fred Fredericks, conga player Smiley de Jonnes, drummer Julian Bahula and vocalist Princess Audrey. The name of Dudu's present band is Zila which means, 'We are Here'.

Many South African musicians

Johnny Dyani

who have worked with Dudu in the past are now running their own bands. Johnny Dyani is in Denmark with his group Witch-doctor's Son. Louis Moholo is running two bands at the same time, Culture Shock and Spirits Rejoice. Julian Bahula, who went to England in 1973 after running a band in South Africa called Malombo Jazz, is now leading a London-based band known as Jabula.

Waiting for Liberation Day

Due to its rigid apartheid laws, South Africa has lost an enormous amount of musical talent since the sixties — and as a consequence the music scenes of the States and Europe have been enriched, particularly in the field of jazz. These exiled musicians often play in independent Black African countries and many attended and played at FESTAC in Nigeria in 1977 — Jonas Gwangwa, Miriam Makeba, Johnny Dyani, Louis Moholo and Julian Bahula. None of them want to return home to South Africa until Liberation Day.

Music or porridge?

After the exodus of musical talent from South Africa during the 1960s a vacuum was left in the local music scene — a period when watered-down Folk and Rock were fostered by the government. However, local township bands and choirs continued to thrive and literally millions of their records have been produced, usually recorded in backyard studios. This is why all this urban jive is often referred to as 'Mbaqanga Music' — the name for quickly made steamed mealie porridge (i.e. cheaply made records).

It was in the seventies that things began to pick up for the Mbaqanga bands and some of them have become so popular that even South Africa radio plays some of their tunes, though any controversial lyrics are censored.

Some of the top Mbaqanga vocalists today are blind Steve Kekana, and the late Jacob Mpharanyana, whose records, backed by the Cannibals, often sell 50,000 or more. Even more spectacular are the Soul Brothers who have had total record sales approaching the five million mark. Female vocalists are also in demand such as Patience Africa, voted top lady vocalist by the South African Broadcasting Corporation in 1977, and again in 1980. Margaret Singana, SABC's choice in 1978, was the first local artist to receive a platinum disc (sales of 100,000 records).

Back to roots

A new trend is for some of South Africa's top bands to turn back to the Black roots. The Afro-rock band Harari, whose members originally started off in the sixties playing Beatles-type music, now sing about Black awareness. Another Afro-rock band called Era, formed in 1976, had their first album *Manyano* (Unity) banned on South African radio. Also banned was Juluka's single *Africa, The Innocent Weep*, a group put together by a White and a Black musician, Johnny Clegg and Sipho Mchunu.

However, many of these banned songs are being played on the numerous Bantustan radio stations, whose signals can be picked up throughout southern Africa. Another wind of change in the music has come about since Zimbabwe's independence, and the surfacing of local guitar band music there (music influenced by South Africa's township beat, but which uses melodies borrowed from the local hand-piano tradition). Two of the most popular of these sorts of band today are the Shona groups, Oliver and his Black Spirits and Thomas Mapfumu and the Blacks Unlimited, who were both detained under the Smith regime. Another is Dewera Ngawena who plays more in the Zulu style.

So in spite of all attempts to deport musicians and bottle up Black South African musicians — their sounds are coming through loud and clear. A recent sign of European music fans' sudden interest in Mbaqanga is evident — Virgin Records *Rhythms of Resistance*, Rough Trade's *Soweto* compilation album and the Soul Brothers single released by Earthworks Records.

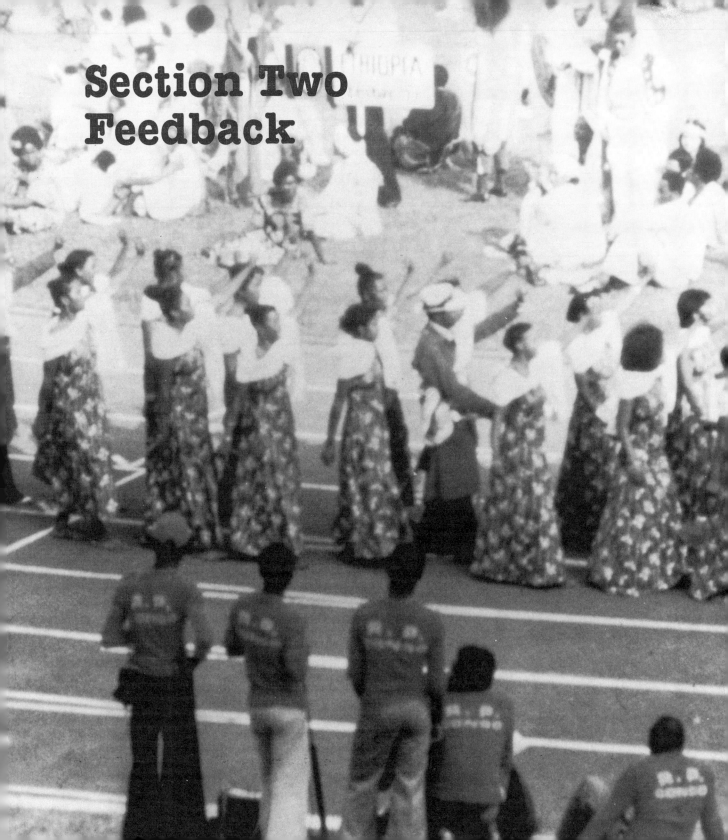

Section Two
Feedback

1 Ragtime to Rumba

Since the end of the nineteenth century, Black music has been prominent in the international arena — from Ragtime to Rumba and Jazz, right up to today's Black and White fusions. Dance music and drama, coming originally from Africa, adapted to the New World creating an enormous impact there, as well as feeding back into the main stream of music in Africa itself. This double transformation in the music, brought about by leaving and returning home has created a truly international music style in Africa, and yet one that is doubly African.

This Black feedback extends far beyond the musical realm. Freed Black slaves from the Americas actually set up towns in Africa, like Freetown in Sierra Leone and Monrovia in Liberia. Brazilian architecture was brought to Africa by ex-slaves from South America. Not to mention a host of Afro-American and West Indian writers, artists and politicians who stimulated African nationalism.

Muscical feedback – Ragtime and Minstrelsy

During the mid-nineteenth century, Caribbean melodies were introduced to Africa by members of West Indian Regimental Bands, stationed in West Africa. This cross-over quickly caught on around the turn of the century, when Ragtimes, Foxtrots and Quicksteps, based on the dance music of North American Blacks, began to hit Africa. Ironically they were introduced mainly by Whites, who had gone crazy over these new

The Accra-based comedians, Williams and Marbel in 1923

73

dance tunes and began disseminating them as sheet music and on old wax cylindrical records.

These re-imported styles were far more popular with African audiences than Western classical music. There is an interesting story of a Belgian colonial officer in the Congo, during this time, who received a box containing a selection of cylindrical records. He would play these for the locals, from time to time, on his wind-up gramophone. The classical pieces left them cold, but they loved the 'trick' ones, in other words Ragtimes and Coon-songs.

When Ragtime hit Africa, it was accompanied by Black Minstrelsy with its tap-dancing and plantation humour. Minstrelsy too had become part of the main stream of European entertainment and was part of the Vaudeville tradition. The whole show was taken to Africa: the records of the Afro-American Vaudeville team of J. Turner Layton and Willie Johnstone, and films of Black and White Minstrels, such as Al Jolson. A live tour of West Africa was even undertaken in the early twenties by the Afro-American man and wife team, Glass and Grant.

By the twenties, Africans were setting up their own Minstrel, Ragtime and Concert Party groups, which performed plays, comedy sketches and dances — the Two Bobs and their Carolina Girl from Ghana; the Dark Town Strutters and Hivers Hivers of South Africa. Another early Minstrel team from Ghana were Williams and Marbel who actually worked with Glass and Grant, before launching off on their own.

Ragtime and Minstrelsy became so popular in Africa, that they were incorporated into local musical, dance and dramatic styles. In Ghana there were the Concert Parties, with their comedian or 'Bob' character. 'Bob' is a combination of the Black minstrel with Ananse, the traditional spider-hero of the Akans. Even the term 'Bob' was an expression that Ghana's original Bob Johnson picked up from visiting Black American seamen, who entertained everyone at dock-side clubs with comedy sketches and dances accompanied by guitarists and banjo players. Highlife absorbed many elements from Ragtime, especially in the coastal towns of Fante, an important location for Ghanaian Minstrelsy.

In South Africa, Ragtime and Honky-tonk piano also became part of the Black urban Marabi music of the twenties and thirties, pounded out on pedal organs in the shebeens (or illegal African drinking bars). Then, at a more refined level, the pianist Reuben Caluzza combined Ragtime with his own Zulu music for choral groups. He was so successful that he was sent to England to record for HMV.

African dance styles come back to Africa

This feedback of Black music from the Americas blew the creative lid off the music scene during the colonial times. It wasn't only North American Ragtime and Minstrelsy that did this, it was also the African-derived dance styles from South America and the Caribbean — the Rumba, Samba,

Conga, Mambo and Meringue, which were already being played by African dance orchestras, and absorbed into the local music, before the Second World War. The Samba, for instance, was introduced to Nigeria by the descendants of freed Brazilian slaves and affected Juju music with its samba drum. Meringue became the national music of Sierra Leone.

Then, in the fifties and sixties, Calypsos, Boleros, Cha Cha Chas, Pachangas and Afro-Cuban percussion became the craze, with the French-speaking African countries going more for Latin-American music and the English-speaking ones for Calypso.

Rumba crazy

One of the earliest and most pervasive of these Afro-Latin and Afro-Caribbean styles is the Rumba, which became an international rage during the thirties. It spread like wildfire in Africa and was incorporated into the local music there during the forties. In East Africa, after the Second World War, African soldiers returning from overseas brought the Rumba with them and set up bands such as the Rhino Boys, ex-soldiers of the King's African Rifles. Another group was led by Lucas Tututu, who composed the famous song *Malaika*, later recorded by Miriam Makeba.

But the Rumba had its biggest impact, and one still felt today, on Zaire and Congo Brazzaville. Even the French and Belgian colonialists used to dance the Rumba, and a local African version of it called N'Goma became popular in French-speaking central Africa.

E.T. Mensah at the Paramount club in Accra

2 Jazz Comes Home to Africa

The Ragtime and Minstrelsy craze in Africa was followed by Dixieland Jazz, which became especially popular in South Africa during the 1920s. Many local Dixie bands were formed there, like the Dark Town Strutters and the Big Four of Johannesburg.

In Ghana, too, Dixieland became part of the repertoire of twenties bands such as the Jazz Kings of Accra. But it wasn't until the fifties that the king of Dixieland Jazz, Louis Armstrong, played live in Africa.

Louis Armstrong plays live in Africa

It all started with Ed Murrow of the Columbia Broadcasting System. He had made a film on Africa in 1955, called *See It Now*. This took him to Accra and to E.T. Mensah's Paramount night-club.

The following year CBS was making a film of Armstrong's European tour and Ed Murrow decided to round off the trip with a visit to Accra by Satchmo (Louis Armstrong) and the All-Stars.

When the musicians and film crew got off the plane, they were welcomed by a massed band of top Ghanaian dance band musicians, and the Nigerian comedian Ajax Bukana, who had played bass for Bobby Benson's band.

That day the All Stars lunched with the Ghanaian Premier, Doctor Kwame Nkrumah, and then performed a free open air show at the Old Polo Ground, to a crowd of over one hundred thousand. In the evening the All Stars played at the Paramount night club, side by side with E.T. Mensah, the King of Highlife. According to the Ghanaian *Daily Graphic* (25 May 1956), the show was a great success.

> E.T. seems to have been inspired by the presence of the great Louis. His fingers moved over the valves of his silver trumpet to produce the best manipulation of this instrument by any West African trumpeter. Louis must have been surprised. He was moved. He was pleased. He went up to E.T. and shook hands with him.

E.T.'s comments on Louis's playing that night are as follows:

> Louis was a great player and put all his energy in, from his head to the tip of his toes. We could see everything quivering, sweating all around and saliva coming out. I observed that if he wanted to play a note, he must force the note to come, come what may. So we could see him pitching high. He found my range and started above it, so that his trumpet sounded like a

Louis Armstrong, his wife Lucille and the Premier of Ghana, Doctor Kwame Nkrumah

clarinet. He was pitching high all the time, his lowest note was my top G. We jammed for about half an hour playing *Saint Louis Blues*. Then he left the stage and listened to us playing highlifes. *'*

The next day the All Stars visited Achimota College and the University at Legon, where they were entertained by traditional African drumming and dancing. At Achimota Louis saw a woman who resembled his mother and he became convinced that Ghana was his ancestral home. That evening they played at a charity show at the Opera Cinema which the Premier Doctor Nkrumah attended. E.T. has some comments on this show too.

' When the show started there was scarcely any applause. The music was thin for us Africans and we wanted more rhythm. For about the first four numbers, when they finished the audience would just look at them. The people had not known how to give heavy applause at the end of the music as is done abroad. So the musicians were getting no encouragement. It was Trummy Young, the trombonist, who saved the situation. He played reclining on his back using his legs to move the slide and he got a huge applause for this. This raised the morale of the public and the musicians and from then on people became interested. The show didn't close until nearly midnight. *'*

The All Stars enjoyed Ghana so much that their clarinetist Edmund Hall, returned the following year and set up a band at the Ambassador Hotel in Accra. Louis himself returned for a visit in 1962. By then many of the top dance bands in Ghana were playing Dixieland numbers, like *Tiger Rag* and *Saint Louis Blues*. *All for you*, the song that welcomed the All Stars at the Accra Airport, shows the inseparable link between Black American and African music. For Ghanaians it was one of

Louis Armstrong and the All Stars welcomed at the airport in Accra by Ghanaian musicians and a Nigerian comedian

their old Highlife songs, but Satchmo remembered it as an old Creole song from the southern states of America.

Randy Weston – Afro-American Jazz Pianist returns to roots (interview with Sylvia Moore)

The same extraordinary re-awakening was experienced by Randy Weston, another famous musician, born of the Black American Jazz scene, or African Rhythms, as Randy prefers to call it. Randy spent several years in Africa exploring his heritage. Now, he is a musical gypsy moving between Africa, Europe and the Americas. In an exclusive interview at FESTAC in 1977, with Sylvia Moore, Randy had this to say about his African rediscovery:

Sylvia: When did you first visit Africa, Randy?

Randy: 15 January 1961, I believe, Lagos, Nigeria.

Sylvia: What made you come to Africa?

Randy: Well, tremendous interest and a desire to come to Africa. I came over with 28 other artists from the United States to see what the relationship was between the art of West Africa, the music of West Africa, literature, painting, sculpture, and the art of Black America.

Sylvia: What did you find?

Randy: I found tremendous similarities — similar faces, expressions, movements, dance steps. They had a group, from the country, come in and dance. It was amazing to see the similarities in the steps.

Sylvia: You eventually came to live in Africa; how did people in New York react to this venture of yours?

Randy: Well a lot of people thought I was out of my mind, 'What are you going to Africa for?' and what

not. Some other people understood, and thought it would be a fantastic change for me, because I had a tremendous desire to live in Africa, because I like to be so close to this wonderful music, and that's the best way to do it.

Sylvia: What kind of discoveries did you make then, in the field of music?

Randy: Well the first discovery, I think, and the most important discovery was that I suddenly realised after hearing the various types of music that we in the United States were just simply an extension of Africa, being like almost the beginning of life itself and like it's thrown itself out in different parts of the world. So I heard music that sounded like everything from Louis Armstrong to Bessie Smith. I just heard everything we do in its true form, I guess. So I think that was a tremendous discovery for me, and from that discovery I started performing with ethnic musicians in Morocco and Sénégal and I found myself playing almost poly-rhythmically, as a pianist; I began to influence my own style of music. I want to mention my son, because he had gone to Africa when he was fifteen years old, and he studied, travelled and listened to the indigenous drummers, and when he returned to the States everybody thought he was really fantastic, because he has a concept that's fantastic, and I explained the reason for that is because he listened and studied with the great drummers of Africa.

Sylvia: You give concerts together with your son now?

Randy: Yes, when we can get together. He works with Dizzy

Gillespie, when Dizzy Gillespie has a big band. He just came from Japan, with a Japanese pianist, that's why he's not here with me in Lagos. Whenever we can get together, we'll get together. I hope we can get together this summer, because I may perform with a group at several festivals in Europe and he may join me.

Sylvia: You said to me that 'music is the true gift'. Did you find that this made it easy for you to travel in Africa and communicate with people?

Randy: Africa, and all over the world, all over the world. Sometimes when you play music and it's music, you know it's entertaining, people will applaud; if you play well, you'll usually be treated nicely by people all over the world, because almost everybody likes music, really. If you play well, people are very, very receptive to music. But I've discovered, since performing in lands and countries where I didn't speak the language and didn't know the customs, I found out that I was able to communicate in a tremendous way with the people, and then it really shows that music is really our first, first language, and it's a good language to return to, because it's a language that all the people on the earth can communicate with.

Sylvia: What would you say, then, are the most important things that African music can contribute to you?

Randy: African music has contributed much to me. When we look at the Western hemisphere, the music of the Western hemisphere has influenced quite a bit of the whole world, what with the Bossanova in Brazil, Calypso in Trinidad and Jamaica, what they call Jazz, Gospel, Pop or Blues in the United States. One looks at the Western hemisphere and discovers all these types of music, which are really fairly new in the history of music.

You find out that in every case, this music has come from African people, maybe two or three hundred years away, but two or three hundred, or four hundred years is only a pinpoint in time. It's really no time at all, for when one thinks about time, we're talking about thousands of years. So to answer your question, what African music means to me, it means that I play African music, it means that I'm a product of African culture. It means that when I was a boy, and my father insisted that I took up classical piano, I used to suffer, turn the clock ahead, and try to sneak out of the window and play basketball, or football. I suddenly realised that this music wasn't natural for me, and that's why I rejected it. This went on for three years, until finally the teacher told my father, 'This boy will never play the piano, you know he never will.' Then when I started playing on my own, I suddenly realised what it was.

Sylvia: It came from within you?

Randy: Yes, of course.

Sylvia: So in fact you taught yourself to play, or did you listen to other musicians?

Randy: Oh, I listen about twenty-four hours a day, because at about that time it was live music everywhere, just three o'clock, four o'clock, five o'clock in the morning, our clubs would start, till ten o'clock the next morning. So there was music constantly, I listened like crazy, and stopped very close to musicians I loved, and got to know them and meet them. But it's like a spiritual door. It's like when you discover, when you say to yourself, which is what my father said to me, 'Son, you're born in Brooklyn, I'm from Panama, Jamaica, your mother's from Virginia, but don't forget we're African people, and you're an African. One day you've got to return to where you've come from, then you'll understand many things about yourself, about me, about your mother, about your culture'; and the old man was right.

Sylvia: Do you think then that African peoples, peoples of African descent from the United States and other places, are getting closer together now?

Randy: They're getting closer together spiritually, and what I mean by that is that I feel that there are forces that are beyond us, that are bringing us together; but there is so much to be done; to do this, it's going to be a long process, I think. But I think spiritually, yes, it is happening. There is a tremendous need for people today; they want to know more about Africa. The history books are slowly being changed. So I think there's a natural spiritual process now of Africa reasserting itself, just like the Arab world is asserting itself. I think we're just going through that change of civilisation.

Sylvia: What would you say then are the most exciting trends you've seen, now that you've come back to Africa?

Randy: Well for me again, it's that spiritual movement; O.K. now, there were problems here of organisation, but almost every festival I've ever been involved with has had tremendous problems of organisation, so that doesn't surprise me, in the least. But to see a building like that, for African and for Black arts, a beautiful, modern, magnificent theatre, not perfect (but few places are) but dedicated to African and Black arts, to me this is a major spiritual movement, and so that is the level as I see it, way beyond anything else.

Sylvia: What about the future, are you going to continue living in France and commute to Africa regularly, or live in Africa?

Randy: No, I feel that Africa is where I must live, sooner or later. But with the nature of my work, I will always be travelling, that cannot be helped. But I will return to Africa, because I like the life, I like the people, and I like the challenge, because to search for the ancient culture and the ancient music, to me, is much more exciting than trying to get to the moon, because it's a very heavy spiritual mystery for modern man today. Everybody's getting interested in Africa, doctors are — how certain people use music for healing purposes, for therapy; I think Africa now is the most exciting place in the world, because the rest of the world is becoming so mechanical.

Sylvia: What do you think that your music does to people?

Randy: Well, I like to think that my music will have people, after they leave the concert or whatever, think about Africa and Africa's people on a different kind of level.

Randy Weston

79

Part of a river reggata at FESTAC

3 Soul to Soul

The influence of Rock and Roll on the African music scene

In the early sixties the international pop revolution reached Africa in the form of Rock and Roll. Rock and Roll is nothing more than a commercialised version of Rhythm and Blues, Soul music created in the forties by American Blacks who had migrated to the cities.

Not suprisingly, Rock and Roll, even though mainly played by White musicians, struck a vibration with the African youth, who started to play the music of Elvis Presley, Fats Domino and Cliff Richard. One of the first African Pop bands was the Heartbeats of Sierra Leone, formed in 1961 by Geraldo Pino. This band was to change the face of the music scene on the West African Coast. Many student bands were formed in Sierra Leone taking their cue from the Heartbeats, for example the Echoes, Golden Strings and Red Stars.

During the mid-sixties there was a fertile Pop scene much of which centred around the Yellow Diamond night-club in the capital Freetown, run by a band called the Leone Stars. Here's how Samuel Oju King, an ex-member of the Echoes, describes it.

> The Leone Stars was formed out of the break-up of two visiting bands, Outer Space from Nigeria and a Ghanaian band based at the Tijuana night-club in Freetown. They all teamed up with a Sierra Leonese conga player, then obtained a loan and renovated a vacant club, formerly known as the Swazark Club. Progressive music like Jazz and Pop was played at the Yellow Diamond, and on Saturday afternoons they had jam-sessions featuring prominent musicians. For instance, there was a Black American musician called Woodie who was a diplomat. Another was a Ghanaian drummer called Buddy Peep who had been in the United States playing Jazz.

The musicians who congregated around this club also instigated a twelve-hour jam-session at the Juba Barracks, just outside Freetown. Fourteen bands played at this, mainly from Sierra Leone, but there was also one band from Guinea and the Formulas from England.

Rock in Ghana

The first Pop group in Ghana was formed by a group of soldiers who were members of an army band called the Red Devils. After training in England, where they were exposed to the music of Cliff Richard and the Shadows, they

returned to Ghana and formed the Avengers, in 1962. Within a few years there were dozens of student Pop bands playing the music of the Beatles, Rolling Stones and Spencer Davis. Bands like Ricky Telfer's Batchelors and the Sharks, both from Achimota College — and others like the Road Runners, Blues Syndicate, Circuit Five and the Phantoms. All vied for first place at the countless school Pop chains, or Pop competitions, organised by impressarios like Raymond Azziz and Faisal Helwani.

Rock in Nigeria

In Nigeria it was the same story, with student bands in Lagos like Yinka Balogun's Rock and Roll outfit, the Spiders; the Cyclops with their bell-bottomed trousers and Chuck Berry music; and the Clusters, hailed as Africa's Beatles (Joni Haastrup of the Clusters has become one of Nigeria's leading Rock musicians). Another was Segun Bucknor's Hot Four, formed with the Nelson Cole brothers. Here is what Segun has to say about Nigerian rock bands:

> Rock and Roll bands were school bands and the first one was the Blue Knights. Then the first serious one we saw was the Cyclops; they were just out of school and were formed in 1964. The beginning of Pop and Rock and Roll was at the United States Information Service, as they had an amplifier and a PA. We used to go there at weekends, but as there were no permanent groups we would just team up and give ourselves a name.

The opening parade at FESTAC

Geraldo Pino

The parents of these kids, of course, hated all this, and something of a generation gap developed between the old and young with pop as one of the sore issues. Up to the mid-sixties it was mainly the music of White bands which caught on — Elvis, the Beatles, the Who, the Hollies, the Dave Clarke Five, the Small Faces and the Animals — then all this was overtaken by Black Pop music.

First there was Millicent Small from Jamaica, or 'Millie' as she is generally known, who made two tours of Ghana and Nigeria in 1965 and 1966 introducing West Indian Ska music. Her international hit *My Boy Lollipop* was a big success. Then there was Chubby Checker's *Let's Twist Again*, and everyone went twist crazy, especially in East Africa. Chubby Checker toured Africa in 1966 and 1967. The Nigerians were so impressed that they created their own king of Twist, King Kennytone of the Top Toppers.

The beginnings of Soul

But the biggest wave of Black Pop music to sweep over Africa during these times was undoubtedly Soul which hit Africa well before it hit Europe. In fact it was Liberia, with its American-Liberians, who first got Soul.

However, Liberia didn't produce Africa's first band to play the music of James Brown, Wilson Pickett, Otis Redding and Ray Charles. This band came from Sierra Leone, Geraldo Pino's Heartbeats who left Freetown in 1964 and spent two years in Monrovia. They then spent two years spreading Soul music in

Ghana. In 1968 Chris Okotie took them to Lagos where they dominated the Nigerian Pop scene for a good two years. They've now split up. Those who stayed in Lagos with Francis Foster formed Baranta, whilst Pino himself shot up to Kano where he formed the New Heartbeats with the Plastic Jims from Ghana.

The Heartbeats created a wake of Soul bands wherever they went in the late sixties. Ghana's first Soul group was the El Pollos led by Stan Todd and Elvis J. Brown and others soon followed. King Bruce's old Black Beats dance band went over to Soul in 1969 when the youthful Sammy Odoh (Owusu) and Ray Otis took over. Another band especially created by King Bruce to cater for Soul music was the Barbecues led by Tommy Darling.

In Nigeria, the influence of the Heartbeats affected many of the Pop bands, like the Clusters and Hykkers which went overboard for Soul, and Joni Haastrup, who became Nigeria's James Brown. Then Tony Benson, son of the famous old-time band leader Bobby Benson, set up the Strangers who played at his father's night-club in Lagos, the Caban Bamboo.

Another Soul freak was Segun Bucknor who, in 1968, after a two-year trip to the States, shaved off all his hair, teamed up again with the Nelson Cole brothers and formed Segun Bucknor and his Soul Assembly. It was this group that released popular records like *Lord Give Me Soul* and *I'll Love You No Matter How*.

By 1969 Segun was fusing Soul with African music and generally

Tee Mac, leader of the Afro-collection

becoming more and more original. He changed the name to Segun Bucknor and the Revolution and released a string of controversial songs like: *Son of January 15th* a poetical history of modern Nigeria; *Who Say I Tire*, a satire on modern life in Lagos; and *Pocket your Bigmanism* against the nouveau riche of Nigeria.

Even in French-speaking Zaire, soul music became popular and musicians started to produce their own local versions of it. Most well known is *Sukki Sy Man*, an archetypal Soul number that became a smash-hit in West Africa in the late sixties.

So, by copying pop music, first White and then Black, creative young African musicians turned back to their own sources of energy. For the Blacks the influx of Soul brought its messages of 'doing your own thing' and 'Black and proud'. This trend was accelerated by the impact of the ultra-creative and psychedelic rock of Jimi Hendrix, Cream and Santana.

One of the first African bands to play this freak-out music was the Super Eagles of Gambia (now known as Ifang Bondi and the Afro-Mandingue Sounds) which toured West Africa in the late sixties. In 1968 they visited Ghana where underground bands like the Aliens, Barristers and Blue Magic were formed. The psychedelic Aliens released an EP that combined African music with Jimi Hendrix-type guitar playing. Then in Nigeria there was the Afro-collection which was formed in 1971 with some of today's leading musicians in Nigeria, like the leader Tee Mac,

The massed horsemen of Kano at FESTAC

Berkely Jones, Laolu Akins, Mike Odumosu and Joni Haastrup.

The period from 1969 to 1971 was one where musicians got away from the 'copyright' mentality of simply copying Western pop music. When Soul crossed over to Africa, young musicians made a quantum leap out of the copy-cat strait-jacket. Here's what Segun Bucknor says about his band Revolution, formed in 1969:

After the Assembly I changed the name to Revolution as I was experimenting with Pop music but using the real basic African beat, the African jungle-beat which we call the Kon-kon, in 6/8 time. We did something like Santana did with Latin music and pop. Before Santana there were Latin American groups that were making it, but not that big. But since Santana came out with a Rock-Latin beat, the older Latin-American musicians are coming up, like Mongo Santamaria who's a bongo player. You know Latin-American music and our music is virtually the same. It's all in 6/8 time but when you play Latin-American music you have to double the tempo.

1971 Soul to Soul concert

It was at this time that Fela in Nigeria began his Afro-beat and Ghana's Osibisa, based in London, burst into the European market with their Afro-rock. Another stimulus to the creative scene, this time in Ghana, was the Soul to Soul concert held in 1971. It was a massive two-day event at which top Black American bands played side by side with Ghanaian groups. Tens of thousands flocked to Accra's Black Star Square. This unique happening was recorded and later released on film and record.

There were American artists like the gospel singer Roberta Flack, the ghetto music of the Voices of East Harlem, the Staple Singers with father and daughters, Soul singers like Ike and Tina Turner and Wilson Pickett. One of the policemen who was on duty for the show got so excited by Wilson Pickett that he jumped up on stage and started dancing with his hero, mindless of his uniform. (Ghana's police and army took a special delight in Soul music and have their own Soul bands, such as the Black Berets of the Recce Regiment.) Ghana's own top Soul group, the El Pollos, also performed at this memorable show, as did the grandad of Ghanaian Palm-Wine music, Kwaa Mensah.

New creations were also in the air and Ghana's Kofi Ghanaba (Guy Warren) played way-out drum solos backed by a full choir. Another performance that crackled with energy and new vibrations was the Afro-American Jazz group of Les McCann and Eddie Harris. They teamed up with Amoah Azangeo, master of the Fra-fra calabash of northern Ghana. Unlike the maraccas which are simply shaken, this Fra-fra instrument is thrown around the body in a sort of juggling act providing the framework for the complex rhythms of Amoah's songs. The scintillations created by this combination of Fra-fra and

Afro-American music had to be heard to be believed, and fortunately can still be heard on the *Soul to Soul* record album. Following exposure to the international arena, Amoah launched out on an experimental phase. Up to then he had been playing his local music for the Ghana Arts Council, but after his Soul to Soul experience he joined up with the Afro-rock band, Basa-basa.

The music that made the deepest and most long-lasting impression on the Ghanaian music scene during this marathon show was, however, Santana's. Their combination of Latin-American music and Rock became a source of inspiration for a generation of young Ghanaian musicians who went on to do the same thing with African music and Rock.

So with Fela and Segun Bucknor doing their thing in Lagos, Osibisa doing their's in London and the Soul to Soul concert staged in Ghana, around the turn of this decade a profusion of Afro-fusion bands appeared — BLO, Monomono, Ofo and Ofege from Nigeria and Boombaya, the Zonglo Biiz, Hedzolleh, Sawaaba Soundz and the Big Beats of Ghana: bands that dominated the local Pop market in the mid-seventies.

FESTAC

However, the biggest Soul to Soul experience of the seventies was undoubtedly FESTAC, the Second World Black and African Festival of Arts and Culture, held in Nigeria in 1977. FESTAC brought together the traditional and contemporary arts of the eight hundred million Blacks living throughout the world in Africa, the New World and Melanesia.

This one thousand million pound spectacular was attended by Black delegations from sixty-two countries. Events included a traditional durbar, reggatas and performing arts from the host country, Nigeria. A colloquium on Black civilisation was attended by seven hundred scholars. There were fifty plays, one hundred and fifty music and dance shows, eighty films, two hundred poetry and literature sessions and forty art exhibitions.

It would be impossible to list all the music and dance events, but here are a few: from African countries there were Miriam Makeba, Osibisa, Bembeya Jazz, Les Amazones, the Golden Sounds, Louis Moholo and Dudu Pukuwana; from the Caribbean, the Mighty Sparrow and the Cuban National Dance Troupe; from Latin-America, Omo Alakuta and her Yoruba/Brazilian priestesses and Gilberto Gil's Afro-Latin music; from North America, Stevie Wonder, Sun-ra, Donald Byrd and the Blackbyrds; from Australia and New Guinea, Aborigine dances.

'FESTAC 77 was an unprecedented confluence in human history. The African and Black world organised it for their own people, providing them with opportunities for self-realisation, discovering a sense of the past, and preparing for the future. FESTAC was an immense building site where work had yet to start, a flickering light on the ocean. The flow to the source had made it possible to formulate realistic plans for progress, based on the inter-dependence of cultural, political and economic growth. The merging of the ways had enriched and inspired thousands of people.'

(Moore, The Afro-Black Connection, 1977)

The National Theatre built for FESTAC in Lagos

Section Three
Cross-overs

Ginger Johnson (playing squeeze drum) and his African drummers with the Rolling Stones

1 Africa Goes West

Most people know that Jazz, Blues and Latin-American music partly came from Africa, but most do not realise that these dance styles were not only taken back to Africa, where they became incorporated into the local music scenes there, but that these local fusions then crossed back over the Atlantic.

There are many early examples of these cross-overs of modern African music and its musicians. For instance, the Gold Coast Police Band introduced live Highlife music to England in the late thirties, during the coronation of King George the Sixth. Then, in the forties and fifties, African musicians played with top American and British dance bands and naturally enough pushed their own local music. Two of these were the Ghanaian Caleb Quaye and Guy Warren who played drums for Kenny Graham's Afro-cubists in London and then introduced 'Afro' music to the States. Another was the late Ginger Johnson, a Nigerian drummer who played with the Edmundo Ross Band and later set up his own African drum orchestra and the Iroqo Club in London.

In today's Pop world this process has gathered momentum and many African artists have a base in Europe and the States, visit these countries, and release records abroad.

Many of the great names have already appeared in this book, but now we turn to another great name, Guy Warren, whose Afro-jazz fusions made a big impression on Afro-American music in the 1950s. Then to the 'roots' music of today, especially Rasta and Reggae music which is acting as a stepping stone back to Africa. Thirdly we look at New Wave for,

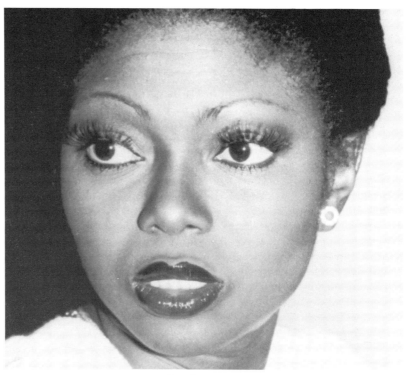

Patti Boulaye

believe it or not, even this music is unconsciously acquiring an African touch, for when they adopt

the beat of the West Indian rude-boys, African-type cross-rhythms emerge.

Gasper Lawal

2 Guy Warren, the Original African Cross-over

One of the earliest and most famous of these cross-over musicians is the Ghanaian ace drummer Guy Warren, or Kofi Ghanaba as he is now called. In his early days he was much influenced by Jazz and took his Afro-jazz fusions to America in the fifties, where they really caught on with Black Americans. He met and played with most of the top Black Jazz musicians in the States and was one of the influences that turned them back to their African roots.

I first met Ghanaba in 1974 at his palatial home built from the royalties from his record releases. Being in advance of his times in every way, he was one of the first African musicians to get his songs copyrighted. Today he is a rather mysterious figure who likes being on his own and derives his spiritual powers from his drumming and his Buddhist faith.

Ghanaba was born in Accra in 1923 and from early on in life became interested in drums, both local percussion and Jazz drumming.

We lived in downtown Accra where they had this bar that catered for seamen, prostitutes and pimps. They had a combo there and we could hear them from where we were living. They played Ragtimes. I learnt to tap-dance and there was this great drummer who died, Harry Dodoo, a Jazz drummer who used to juggle with the sticks and joke, just like Baby Dodds. He was my hero. Also, in my house, there were some Ewe people and every Saturday night they would hold a traditional drum session, for they are a very musical tribe. We used to have masquerade parades in Accra every Christmas and everybody would do a sort of poor man's quadrille to the sound of the bass drum, flute and pati-drum.

For a time, Ghanaba was a member of the Accra Rhythmic Orchestra but found its music too 'ballroomish'. So, just after the Second World War, he joined the famous Tempos dance band of E.T. Mensah. Ghanaba not only brought his excellent Jazz drumming to this band, but he also introduced Afro-Cuban percussion instruments, since he had played with Kenny Graham's Afrocubists in London for a time.

But Jazz was Ghanaba's first love. According to E.T., he was so fanatical about Jazz, that when the Tempos were playing a Highlife or Foxtrot, Ghanaba would only play half-heartedly, keeping all his energy back for the Jazz numbers. Ghanaba developed a perfect American accent, which as he explains, once got him into trouble at the European Club in Accra:

During the intermission I went over to see a White guy. This guy's Canadian friend said, "What's an American nigger doing here?" He thought I was an American and I thought he was one. He pushed me and I saw red and thrashed his arse out. You see this was the sort of club where Africans were only seen padding about gently, dressed in white tunics and here I was beating this guy up. It was a sensation.

Ghanaba left the Tempos in 1950 and spent a few years in Liberia as a radio disc jockey. Then he made his way to America with the intention of playing Jazz. But as he describes, it did not work out quite like that, for when he got there he realised:

I could never play like Gene Krupa, Max Roach or Louis Bellson. They have a different culture. So I had to make a choice of being a poor imitation of Buddy Rich or playing something they couldn't. So I started to play African music with a little bit of Jazz thrown in, not Jazz with a little African thrown in. For it is African music that is the mother, not the other way around. But I had to find out the hard way!

It was in Chicago that he met his muse who was to be 'the African musician who re-introduced African music to America to get Americans to be aware of this cultural heritage of Black people.' It was from this time that he produced a series of revolutionary albums like *Africa Speaks, America Answers, Theme for African Drums, African Sounds, Third Phase* and *Afro-jazz*.

Ghanaba anticipated many of the 'Afro' and 'root' trends of the seventies and the present generation of Black musicians. In many ways he is their spiritual father and that is why Ghanaba is so critical of musicians who only go in for copying other people. He has gone through the whole process himself — of leaving home in search of a new sound and ending up coming back home.

Since the late sixties he has been based in Ghana, and has been helping to develop the local music scene, and collecting a vast archive on Black music from all over the world. He also played at the meeting of Black American and African musicians at the Soul to Soul concert held in Accra in 1971.

His son, Glen Warren, is a well-known drummer, and recently father and son released an album.

Ghanaba was far ahead of his time. The rise of African music to an international level, that he has struggled for all these years, is now well under way. But I should like the famous Afro-American jazz drummer, Max Roach, to have the last word on Ghanaba's contribution to Black music. In a letter written in 1973, he says,

In this letter I would like to record that Ghanaba was so far ahead of what we were doing (in the fifties) that none of us understood what he was saying — that in order for Afro-American music to be stronger, it must cross-fertilise with its African origins. Ghanaba's conception, like that of Marcus Garvey, George Washington Carver etc., was beyond our grasp. We ignored him. Seventeen years later Black music in America has turned to Africa for inspiration and rejuvenation and the African sounds of Ghanaba are now being played all over the United States, wherever Afro-American music is played.

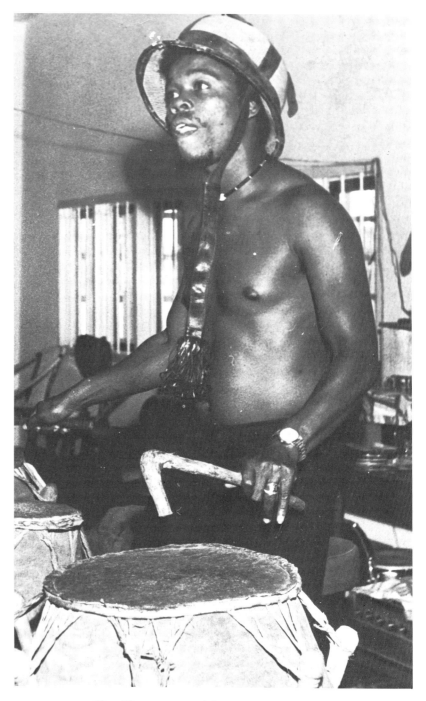

Glen Warren, son of Ghanaba (Guy Warren)

90

3 Roots, Rasta, Reggae – Stepping-stones Back to Africa

The optimistic sixties, with their psychedelia, flower power and 'you've never had it so good' boom days, have long passed away. In the West, 'progress' is no longer taken for granted. On the one hand it is no longer automatic because of limited resources, and because the claims of the underprivileged world to their primordial human rights, and to a fair division of the world's resources. On the other hand, the negative effects of progress through over-mechanisation, cannot be turned off. These negative effects include technological determinism, squandering of resources, industrial serfdom and redundancy. This has led to a basic questioning of the tenets of technological civilisation and a re-evaluation of cultural traditions because cultural heritage and cultural identity are the bases for self-determination and development. An example of this quest is the immense success of Afro-American Alex Haley's book *Roots* which traces his ancestors all the way back to Africa and looks at what happened in the New World.

But the biggest upsurge of this 'back to Africa' identity and heritage theme has come from the Caribbean, with its Reggae music, preaching the doom and downfall of Babylon, i.e. Western civilisation. Reggae is the most recent of a number of Jamaican dance-styles following the Calypsos and Mento of the colonial period. The first of these new styles was Ska or Blue beat, fast dance music in which the rhythm of Calypso was combined with Black American Rhythm and Blues — but with the beat turned inside out. The biggest commercial success of this music was Millicent Small's *My Boy Lollipop*, Chris Blackwell's first Island Record success, released in the early sixties. By the mid-sixties this tune had become so well-known that Millie made two tours of Africa.

Ska was followed in the late sixties by a slowing down of the beat to Rock Steady, played by bands like the Heptones and artists like Ken Boothe.

Around 1970 the tempo speeded up a little into Reggae, whose main artists are Desmond Dekker, Jimmy Cliff, Toots and the Maytals, Peter Tosh and the Wailers and, of course, until recently, Bob Marley. This music now dominates the world music market.

Linked with the waxing of Reggae music was the surfacing of the Jamaican millenarian cult, Rastafarianism, a cult of protest against discrimination. The collapse of the over-complex Western world is forecast and followers are urged to return to their roots and a simpler way of life. This Ethiopian Christian church is based on the beliefs of Jamaican Marcus Garvey, who in the 1920s predicted that a King of Kings would be crowned in Africa. This would be the signal for the downfall of the West and the repatriation of Blacks to Africa.

This prediction seemed to come true when Haile Selassie was made Emperor, King of Kings, and the Lion of Judah in 1930, and later when the Italian colonialists were defeated. The word Rastafarian comes from the royal title of Haile Selassie, Ras Tafari. It was also widely believed that Selassie was the leader of a secret society called the Nyabingi. Members of this society had long matted hair, used Ganja as a sacrament and were dedicated to overthrowing White and Black oppressors. The 'dread locks' of the Rastas were copied from these 'nyamen', as the West Indians call them.

By the fifties there were Rasta communities all over Jamaica and their spiritual music, dance and chants were played on hand drums and rumba boxes. The Rastas reached a state of possession, or 'high', through their music and through 'trumping' — rhythmic deep breathing. Thus disorientation of the everyday perceptions, leads to heightened perception, and therefore, to transformation.

It is the religious music of Rasta that has so deeply influenced Reggae, turning it into the apocalyptic roots Reggae of Bob Marley and the Wailers.

In spite of all opposition, reggae music and the Rastafarian faith have not only flourished in their birthplace, but in Europe as well, the very heart of Babylon, where the first industrial revolution took place. In Britain, where many West Indians were invited to settle in the fifties with the hope of a bright future, these immigrants saw their children condemned to unemployed life in city ghettos like Saint Paul's in Bristol, Notting Hill in London and Toxteth in Liverpool — the very places where the youth, spear-headed by Blacks, has gone on the offensive against the police. At the Notting Hill Jamaican Carnival in London, attracting half a million tourists, violent clashes between youths and the police have occurred several times, although recent carnivals have been peaceful. The disillusionment with British life style and establishment is expressed by the poet Linton Kwesi Johnson, born in Jamaica but brought up in Brixton. He has gone back to the African tradition of combining poetry, music and dance with social and political commentary. In his poems like *Dread inna Inglan*, he has become a spokesman for frustrated youth.

Today in the UK not only West Indian youths, but people in general, are becoming more interested in Africa. Information is provided by institutes such as Aklowa House run by the Ghanaian Felix Cobbson, the Iroqo Club of the late Ginger Johnson of Nigeria and the Africa Centre run by the OAU all in London. As a result, in the last few years, a number of bands and dance groups playing Afro-Caribbean music have been set up jointly by West Indians and Africans.

Take Steel and Skin, for example, set up in the mid-seventies by Jamaican born Peter Blackman. This London group combines the music of the Caribbean steel drums with African hand-drums and wooden xylophone, and features traditional African dances.

Steel and Skin

Then, from the Midlands of England, there is Lanzel (Unity) set up in 1978 by an African master drummer together with some unemployed West Indian youths, who were members of a Black self-help organisation called Harambee. There are many other mixed bands, like Ekome, Mystic and the Israelites, Kutamba, Black Velvet, Matta Fancanta, Maas Movers and the Ujaama Players. Ekome (Unity) was formed in Saint Paul's, Bristol in 1977 by Barrington Anderson and his sister Angela, after a series of Steel and Skin workshops.

Originally Ekome was formed by unemployed West Indian youths, but later Ghanaian dancers and drummers came to help them, making them into one of the best Afro-Caribbean groups in the country (they've appeared on TV with Pattie Boulaye). Since 1982 Ekome has been holding its own Arts Festival in Bristol and has also launched an educational programme for school-children. Barrington and company have also helped set up Afro-Caribbean bands elsewhere, like Uzuri Binti from Swindon, the Cardiff Afro-Caribbean Dance Group, Kwame

Nkrumah from Gloucester and the African Arts Project at Derby. Ekome has lately gone electric and has added a full scale dance band to its cultural group, that plays West Indian and African music and features the famous Jamaican trombonist Vinnie Gordon.

Just as with West Indians, these groups are becoming popular with the White youth, as many of the Afro-Caribbean bands are teaching African drumming and dancing in the primary schools.

So Whites have begun to play African music — the Ojah band contains musicians from England and Africa. Then there is the German drum-freak Jojo Wolfe and the Ghanaian guitarist Kris Bediako, creating their Klogo-motion, based on the Kpanlogo rhythm of the Ga's of Ghana. Also from London is Dagarti, a band with musicians from as far afield as Africa, the West Indies, England, Australia and New Zealand.

Even some of the African musicians who came over to the West to play Pop music and Jazz are being infected by the roots movement, for instance Nigeria's Gaspar Lawal, who went to England in the sixties and played with top Rock bands there such as the Rolling Stones and Airforce. In 1980 Gaspar released his *Ajomase* album which prominently features traditional African percussion and the Kora, a harp-lute.

So whether it's the roots, Jazz or Afro-American bands like Sun Ra and Taj Mahal, the Rasta and Reggae music of the West Indies, or the mixed Afro-Caribbean bands of Europe, all eyes and ears are now on Africa.

It is not at all surprising, then, that West Indian music, particularly Reggae, has crossed back over to Africa and top stars like Jimmy Cliff, Eddy Grant and the late Bob Marley have made tours there.

Reggae in Africa

Reggae is having an immense impact on the modern African music scene and has been copied by many local musicians there. This process is now leading to the emergence of African Reggae which is

The Afro-Caribbean group, Ekome

feeding back into the international Reggae scene.

The most well known Afro-reggae star is Sonny Okosun, whose albums *Papa's Land* and *Fire in Soweto* have been released by EMI in the international market. But there are many others. For instance, Nigeria's Highlife superstar Victor Uwaifo has experimented with Jamaican music on tracks like *When the Sun Shines* and *Five Days a Week Love*. Ghana's top guitar band, the African Brothers, has done the same, in the release *None but You*, combining Highlife and Reggae. Bongo's Ikwue also plays Reggae numbers.

Then there is the Liberian singer Miatta Fahnbulleh's song *Koko-rioko*, a Reggae/traditional song that she has released as a twelve-inch single. Also released as a twelve-inch disco record is an Afro-reggae by a Nigerian band called Cloud Seven, simultaneously released by Otis Brothers in Africa and Europe. Gaspar Lawal's roots album *Ajomase* contains a Reggae track entitled *Kita Kita*.

One of the most successful blends of Reggae and African music has been the brainchild of Rokafil Jazz from eastern Nigeria which used a Reggae type bass-line in its smash hit *Sweet Mother*. This was not only a hit in Africa but also in the Caribbean as well.

So with Reggae music looking to Africa for inspiration, and African musicians playing local versions of Reggae, it is no wonder that the resulting Afro-reggae fusion is breaking all national boundaries and drawing the Pop scenes of Europe, the New World and Africa closer together.

4 Africa and New Wave

Who would have thought that new wave and punk music would turn towards Africa for inspiration, but it is actually happening. Perhaps the West has run out of ideas or wants to get back to a balanced body music again. Maybe it is just the general disillusionment with the so-called benefits of Western civilisation and its negative aspects such as unemployment, pollution, the arms race, and creative disintegration.

New Wave or Punk originally emerged in the mid-seventies as a reaction to the optimism of sixties rock, with its gurus, superstars and stoned-out, passive audiences.

Punk brought this rarefied music down to earth, and got the fans on their feet, dancing to live and immediate music. They did this by getting back to the origins of Rock, the Rock and Roll and Skiffle of the fifties. Rock and Roll itself is a copy of Black Rhythm and Blues, and therefore the punks are copying a copy of Black music.

The lyrics and music of Punk, and the dance and dress of Punk fans demonstrate alienation from roots and the decay of some aspects of Western society, especially in Britain, the birth-place of Punk. As new wave's Laura Logic says, 'Punk is a commitment to ill-health.' With ashen and corpse-like looks, chains on the body and safety pins stuck all over the face, there seems to be a fascination with bondage and the mortification of the flesh. Punk dance is mechanical. All this seems to parody the future world we are heading for — the world of zombies and automatons. Punk's Gary Numan 'deals in images of pain uncertainty and fear' — as a pop reviewer put it. On stage he seals his musicians in transparent plastic cages. The names of Punk bands and titles of their hit songs are a reminder of Punk beliefs — *Ashes to Ashes*, *Grey Days*, *UK Decay*, *Don't Stand too Close to Me*, *Paranoia*, the Police, Concrete Jungle, Nuclear Summer and Dead Kennedy's.

Two-Tone

Unemployment and decay are particularly evident in Britain's industrial Midlands, where New Wave's shift to Black roots came about. It started in 1978 when the Two-Tone phenomenon was launched by the Coventry-based band, the Specials. This mixed Black and White band fused White Punk lyrics with Black Ska and Reggae music. Many groups have followed suit — such as the Beat, Madness, Body Snatchers, Selector, Swinging Cats and UB40.

As Selecter's Neol Davies says, 'This world tries to separate everything, but Two-Tone means non-separation and bringing together, seeing things in their entirety. Thus, Two-Tone is proving that Black and White can work together harmoniously in Britain.'

Today this Black and White fusion reflects a growing interest in Afro-Caribbean and African music. For instance, Dave Steele of the Beat calls his music 'psychedelic Calypso'. The band's Black saxist, Saxa, specialises in Tangos, Mambas and Cha Cha Chas. The Beat's two guitarists use the African technique of cross-rhythms and 'inside rhythms'. According to Dave Wakelin, the band's White guitarist, who is left-handed, 'Andy, the Jamaican guitarist, and I get cross-rhythms going — me going down while he's going up — and these create a third rhythm of their own.'

Vaughan Tru of the Swinging Cats is moving his Two-Tone sound from Ska to the Bossanova. In 1980 the Piranhas group got as far as number five in the British top twenty, with their Punk version of the South African Jive *Tom Harke*. Many English kids began to whistle this catchy tune without realising it was from Africa. The Specials and Bombay Duck started using African-type clip rhythms in some of their songs, in 1980.

This trend in New Wave has continued. Adam and the Ants and Bow-wow-wow have used Burundi drumming from East Africa in some of their hits and Johnny Rotten's band, Public Image, uses North African drums. When I visited the home of Ian Dury of the Blockheads, I discovered that he is building up a collection of Fela Aníkúlápo-Kuti's albums.

One recent reviewer of the Police said that this band has 'an African feeling, being ardent exploiters of gaps in music, always emphasising the bits around the beat, rather than the beat itself'. Selector actually has two African members, their Ghanaian-born guitarist Compton Amanor, and the vocalist, Pauline Black who is half Nigerian.

This move towards Africa has

5 Black and White

been recognised by one of new wave's leading lights, the English musician Brian Eno who is based in New York. In a three-page interview in *New Musical Express* in 1980, Brian explained that he has become a fan of Highlife and Fela's Afro-beat because he considered them 'perfect for dancing to, as they leave holes in all the right places'. At the end of 1980, he visited Ghana for three weeks and worked with African musicians there.

What the New Wave musicians and fans appreciate is that music must be danced to and that Africa is Pop's supreme source of dance music. Instead of the deafening and overwhelming sounds of Heavy Metal Rock and extreme forms of Punk, people are now looking for music with holes and space inside. Space within the criss-crossing rhythms giving everyone a chance to create and swing around in that space. Many music fans are fed up with the follow-the-leader approach of watching superstars ego-tripping. Instead of watching passively, they want to get up and participate. They want a balanced music rather than just a wild and loud noise. Punk started off a pure noise, but Two-Tone was a move towards a balance.

It is no wonder that new wave is beginning to turn towards Africa. For African music is body music compelling everybody to participate. African music then has been a balancing factor behind the scenes in Western popular music ever since Ragtime, as African music has space inside for all.

Such a lot's been happening recently in the African music scene of Europe and America that I will finish off this musical cross-over section of the book with a brief look at the African music bands operating in the West, country by country. Some composed solely of Africans, some mixed and a few completely White — like London-based O.K. Jive made up of White

East African guitarists Datsun Cherry and Baron Wayne with Chopper (Bonni Wanda) on bass, Lee Partis on drums and vocalist Ruby Jive.

Britain

Britain is a major focus for African music at the moment, especially since the World Festival of Music

Gasper Lawal

95

The master drummers of Burundi

and Dance (WOMAD), held in 1982 at Shepton Mallet in the West of England, at which many African and Afro bands played, like the Konte Family, a griot group from Gambia who had just released an album on Virgin called *Mandinka Music*.

Then from East Africa came the Master Drummers of Burundi who were featured on a Joni Mitchell album in 1975 called *The hissing of the summer lawns*.

Another traditional African group that played at WOMAD was the Cultural Group from the Dagomba area of northern Ghana.

Highlife superstar Prince Niko from eastern Nigeria was also there, backed by the London-based band, the Ivory Coasters. This band was formed in 1980 by saxophonist Stuart Boardman and guitarists David Draper and Musi Musawi. Musi, from Cameroons, later left to form the Banana Bunch and then the Bushmasters. The Ivory Coasters, with its extra fast brand of Soukous or Congolese music, is still going strong, with Dave and Stuart backed by Martin McManus on percussion, Dave Kenard on drums, Martin Robinson on bass, and George Howder and Claude Deppa (South African) on trombone and trumpet respectively.

Gaspar Lawal also played at WOMAD, with his Drum Oro Band; as did mixed African/West Indian bands like Steel and Skin, Aklowa and Ekome.

British Pop bands with an Afro feel also played at the Festival, like the Beat with their African-like cross-rhythms created out of a blend of Rock and Ska. Then there was King Trigger from Bristol who play a jungle beat. And XTC (Ecstasy) from Swindon who released a song on the WOMAD album called *It's nearly Africa*. This double album, *Music and Rhythm* (released by WEA) contains many songs from the artists who played at the festival plus, in addition, top stars who have been bitten by the African bug, like Brian Eno, David Byrne, Peter Gabriel and Peter Townshend.

One of the most successful London-based African bands at the moment of writing is Orchestra Jazira, which operates from Dalston in North London where it is associated with the Jenako Arts Centre run by Richard Austin.

This band comprises eleven musicians, six African and five White. There's Isaac Tagoe and George Fiawoo on percussion, who came from the London-based Ghanian cultural group run by Felix Cobson (Aklowa). Also from Ghana are the bassist Opata Azu and Kwarkwo Oteng on keyboards. From Sierra Leone there's Follo Graff on rhythm guitar. Martin Nii Moi is one of the more recent members. For many years, he played with the Ghanaian army dance band, the Black Berets (a band in which we both played together in the mid 1970s). English members of Jazira include Nigel Watson on drums, who used to be with the Holloway All Stars, and Ben Mandelson on lead guitar, who helped compile the *Sounds D'Afrique* album for Island Records. Jazira's front line is an all female one with Jane Shorrer (ex-

Thompson Twins) on tenor sax — and on alto Nicky Scott Francis, who has played with South African Julian Bahula and with a feminist band called Jam Today. Finally there's the trombonist 'Fish', a musician, juggler and street performer who played with the women's collective theatre known as Cunning Stunts. Jazira has released one Disco 45 called *Love/Dedevi* (Earthworks label) and with its fusion of Black and White, male and female has built up a large fan club of dancers. But I'll let the bassist Opata have the last say about the group:

❛ We can play many types of music but it's now time for African music to come forward. African music is peace and love and it is international. We are English and African and we want the African to realise that the time for fighting is over — it is time to unite. We want Jazira to be a symbol of our unity. ❜

Also managed by Jenako Arts is the Sierra Leonian band the Super Combo. This group was originally formed in 1975 and had six hits with funky meringues, back home in Sierra Leone. Then disaster hit in London when all their equipment was stolen and they faded out of sight for many years. Now, with the growing interest in African music in London, they have just reformed. The line up of the group is guitars (Emil Ogoo and Len Jones), drums (Sidiku Foster), percussion (Akie Kamara), bass (Lonie Williams) and vocals (Otis Thompson).

Also based in London are the Highlife Internationals, led by guitarist Kwabena Oduro Kwarteng who spent six years with the Ranchis Band of Ghana before going to Britain in 1976. Fellow Ghanaians Ashilley and Herman Asafo-Adjei are on percussion and bass respectively. Then from South Africa comes the saxophonist Frank Williams and drummer Tzu Tzu Mihaly. And from Britain Stuart Harman on trumpet. Highlife Internationals have signed up to do an album with Stern's African Record Centre (Britain's oldest African record shop).

Alpha Waves is another popular London-based Ghanaian highlife band, led by ace saxophonist Ray Allen. Ray was first with the Uhurus dance band of Ghana until 1970, when he came to Britain and played with Traffic, Eddie

Ekome

97

Orchestra Jazira

Quansah and Hi-Tension. Willi Stallibros is the guitarist and he once played for Chilli Willi and the Red Hot Peppers and later Ojah. Ghanaian Kofi Edu is the drummer (he also plays for Pigbag, which he told me he joined because Pigbag's own drummer couldn't stand flying to gigs!).

Also Ghanaian-led is the Afro-rock group Kabbala, formed in 1980 by trombonist Mike Osapanyin and his younger brother Isaac Dankwa Osapanyin (percussion). The bass player Herman Asafo-Adjei is from Ghana, and from Nigeria comes James Mene, the drummer.

One of the group's newest members is Osei Tutu, who until recently was the leader of the Edikanfo band. Edikanfo was the resident group at the Napoleon night-club in Accra, which had some production help from Brian

Eno for their album released in 1981 on Brian's EG label. The only White member of Kabbala is the saxophone player, who is an Australian woman, Louise Elliot. White women playing what are usually considered to be male instruments (i.e. horns) seem to be common with the British African bands, and may have something to do with the fact that horns in African music are played in a receptive and feminine way. Instead of horns blasting out reels of solos, the African horn section punctuates the music and responds to the voices and other instruments. They integrate the music rather than dominate it.

A Disco 45 by Kabbala called *Ashewo Ara* (Afro-rock) *Voltain Dance* (Rock-Agbadza) got into the UK Disco charts in 1983.

Then there's a London-based group led by a Liberian vocalist

called Corinna Flamma. Back in 1969 she, and her three sisters, had a West African hit with their *Bassa Love* release. Then in 1983, with a little help from Nigeria's Gaspar Lawal and Mike Odumosu, she released a single in Britain called *Put your spirit up*, a fusion of New Wave and African music.

A popular six-piece South African/White band resident in London, is Jazz Afrika, led by Julian Bahula. The two other African members are guitarist Lucky Panku and pianist Mervyn Africa. Then Alan Jackson is on drums, Michael Nielson is on flute and sax and on double-bass Roberto Bellatalla.

English Pop bands such as Pigbag, Bow wow wow, Rip Rig and Panic are also being influenced by African music. Another is the Cardiff-based band, Weekend, led by bassist Alison Statton (originally with the Young Marble Giants). Highlife, Congo Jazz and Kwela influences are very noticeable on Weekend's album *La Variété*. Jimmy the Hoover has also been influenced by the African beat.

Finally, before moving away from Britain, I should mention that in 1983 the number of artists from Africa performing there increased dramatically. From Nigeria there was Juju superstar Sunny Ade; from Ghana, Highlife musicians Eric Agyeman and Smart Nkansah; from Zaire, Kanda Bongo Man (who played at WOMAD '83); from South Africa the multiracial Juluka, and from Angola a twenty-five piece band called Semba Tropicana who have just signed up with Atlantic.

Another band that visited Britain in 1983 was the Mandingo Griot Society, which is based in America.

United States

The United States is the home of many South African expatriate musicians like Hugh Masekela and Miriam Makeba. In New York, with its African population estimated at 50,000, there is a lively African music scene at clubs like Club Afrique and the Fez Ballroom. Resident bands in the city are the African Connection made up of Sierra Leonian and Liberian musicians, and a Liberian band called OAU which had a Pan African hit record.

The Mandingo Griot Society, however, is based in Los Angeles and was formed by the Gambian Kora player Foday Musa Suso and a White American percussionist

Alpha Waves

called Adam Rudolph who has played with the Detroit contemporary Jazz Quintet, Eternal Wind and Streetdance. The two of them met in Ghana at the Institute of African Studies at the University of Ghana — and then went to America in 1977 to form the Mandingo Griot Society. There they teamed up with three Afro-American musicians: Joseph Thomas on bass guitar and John Markus on lead/rhythm (both have played with Earth Wind and Fire, Sun Ra and Peter Tosh); then on drums, Hamid Drake, who has toured Africa with the Black American Jazz trumpeter, Don Cherry.

The Mandingo Griot Society have brought out two albums on the Flying Fish label, the first one featuring Don Cherry. Suso also provided some of the griot music for the popular TV series *Roots*, based on the novel by Alex Haley.

France

In Europe the main centre of African music is undoubtedly France, the focus of the French-speaking African record industry and the home of many top African artists, like South Africa's Bongi Makeba, the blind guitarist/poet Pierre Akendengue from Gabon, and musician/writer Francis Bebey from the Cameroons. Cameroonian music is called Makossa, a funked-up version of the traditional 'Abele' wedding parade music and tribal 'Bolo-bo' beat. Many Paris-based artists have had success with this music: Manu Dibango of *Soul Makossa* fame; bassist Vicky Edema, had a big smash in 1981 with his *Thank you Mama* album; and vocalist Rachel who, backed by musicians like Jojo Kouch, Lobé Valery and Mango, stole the show at the Festival des Tropiques in 1982. At the Casino de Paris you

99

Delip Apo and his Afro-Danish group

can hear such bands as the eight-piece group M'bamina which plays Zairean 'Rumba-rock', and Agbavia, led by Kito de Silva of the Republic of Benin, which plays Highlife and Salsa.

Belgium

There's also an interest in African music in Belgium, because of the historical ties between that country and central Africa. For example, the annual Sfinks (sphinx) Festival in 1982 featured artists such as Manu Dibango, Toto Guillaum, Lazare Kenmegre and Francis Bebey from the Cameroons, and Bovick from Zaire.

A result of this has been that some Belgian Pop groups have gone African. Like African Queen from Brussels — an English musician called Sarah Osborne playing with four Belgians and Roland Binde from Zaire. They've all been influenced by Fela Kuti who played in Brussels in 1981.

In other European countries like Germany, Scandinavia and The Netherlands, African sounds are also catching on, particularly since the tours there by Fela Aníkúlápo-Kuti and King Sunny Ade.

Germany

In Germany Griot music has become popular, and successful albums of this music have been produced, like the 1982 release of Bubacar Jammeh. Ghanaian high-life artists like Pat Thomas are also doing well, and in 1983 George Darkoo had a hit with a Disco-Highlife album. Another group operating in Germany is Kapingbdi from Liberia, led by Kojo Samuels and the horn player Maisha, which plays Highlifes, Afro-beats and traditional Liberian music.

Denmark

In 1983 Anglo-African Jazira did a successful tour of Denmark, a country where there are similar mixed bands called Amandu Jaar and Kutarshi (Wake-up).

Kutarshi's line-up includes artists from Ghana, Togo, Sierra Leone and South Africa, as well as Denmark. Delip Apo, the leader, is from northern Ghana. Before coming to Europe, he played with many West African bands. In Ghana he's played with the Vis-à-Vis Pop band and guitar bands like K. Gyasi's, Okukuseku's, Akawaboah's and F. Frempong's; in Sierra Leone with the Afro-Nationals and the Godfathers; in Liberia with Afrodelics and in Ivory Coast the Superstars.

The Netherlands

After the independence of Surinam many Surinam people settled in The Netherlands. Their musical taste and the long-standing interest in Jazz in The Netherlands provided a receptive public for African popular music.

After leaving Osibisa and producing the funk band Hi-Tension, Ghanaian percussionist Kofi Ayivor settled in The Netherlands with his Surinamese wife. Then there are the Gambian musicians who make up Ifang Bondi (to prove oneself) which plays Afro-Mendengue music. This group, formed way back in 1967, was originally known as the Super Eagles of Gambia, and I remember seeing them in Ghana around 1970. At the time they were playing soukous and were well known as the first African band to introduce the wah-wah pedal and fuzz-box. Since then they've gone back to their roots and now play a funky sort of Griot music.

Another way the African-feel is slipping into the Dutch Pop main stream is through the white Ska music of groups like Doe Maar (Do your own thing) and Mark Foggo and the Secret Meeting. These bands are modelled on British Two-Tone bands like the Beat, UB40 and the Specials, and like them have crossed Punk-Rock with Reggae-Ska — creating African-like criss-cross rhythms. Their lyrics are heavily political — again like those of British Two-Tone. Two of Doe Maar's biggest hits in Holland in 1982/3 were De Bomb, about the nuclear bomb and Pa about the dead. According to Stan Rijven, the music reporter of the Trouw newspaper, the reason for Doe Maar's huge success in The Netherlands is that Ska is the best vehicle for singing in the Dutch language and suits it down to the ground — Ska and Dutch go together like Italian and opera do.

In Europe and the States these days it seems that African music is being played by bands of every shade of colour. Pure African bands like Super Combo and M'bamina, West Indian/African fusion groups like Ekome and Steel and Skin, Black and White bands such as Jazira, the Mandingo Griot Society and Jazz Africa — right through to nearly all-White bands.

**Section Four
Roots**

1 Traditional Cool and Hot Rhythms

In spite of slavery and colonialism, African dance music has spread to every corner of the world and is flourishing back home. So what's so special about it? Where does it get its power and popularity?

First and foremost, music in Africa is for everyone, and for every occasion. It is truly folk music played by and for the people.

Wherever you go in Africa, people play and dance — from tiny tots to cool and collected elders.

There is music for all occasions — women pounding yams, a typist putting rhythm into the machine, a plumber embellishing his hammering, and even a traffic policeman pirouetting on his pedestal.

Infants still learn rhythm on their mothers' backs and children have a vast array of musical games and toys. One could say in fact that African music is democratic and that genius and excellence there shine from within the whole community, giving inner illumination and providing the opportunity for tuning in to the world of spirits and of nature. It is alive from within, not dazzling from without, like some of the works of long-dead Western classical composers, or modern rock superstars.

It was this African theme of music for all peoples and all occasions that was taken by slaves to the New World, where it burst asunder some of the strait-jacketing to which Western creativity was subjected.

Another feature of African music which has led to its flourishing in modern times is that it is a unifying body music. There are no disembodied parts. The head is not separate from the feet. So whether in traditional drumming by moonlight, the guitar band music of African night-clubs, or the Funk and Reggae of the discos and sound systems, there is a communion of the beat.

African music brings different aspects of life together since it is performed in association with other art forms such as dancing, drama, masked parades and poetry. Here is a famous poem drummed out by Ashanti drums:

The path has crossed the river,
The river has crossed the path,
Which is the elder?
We made the path and found the
    river,
The river is from long ago,
From the Creator of the Universe.

The tradition of unified art in Africa has continued right up to the present day — one only has to consider the African concert parties in which music, dance, drama, painting and comic literature are fused. In the New World Black Minstrelsy started up and vaudeville with its tap-dancing, Ragtime music, satire and comedy acts. Today there are the toasters and disc jockeys who are this generation's musicians, poets, comedians and commentators — all rolled into one.

The structure of traditional African music

African music unifies by binding together the complicated fragments of a song's cross-rhythms and cross-melodies. First and foremost is the Beat, the rhythmic totality that is repeated in cycles throughout the music.

The separate strands of music are woven together by the use of call and response, dialogue and overlapping conversation between the various rhythms, voices, instruments and dancers — each leaves space for the others. Drummers and dancers may respond to each other; the singer and chorus alternate with one another; and gaps are left open for the participants' handclaps, so everyone has a voice and a sound in the musical happening.

The power of the music

The power of African music and other African arts lies in the fact that they have always been an integral part of life, accompanying all important social functions — weddings, funerals, communal work and play, festivals, religious ceremonies.

African music has a crucial purpose in the transmission of knowledge. There are songs of advice, warning, information and morality. The Ashanti court drummer, or Okyerema, is the actual symbol of knowledge and wisdom. During court cases he drums out council and recommendations. The whole apprentice system is built into African music where the first lesson in becoming a master musician is patience and discipline, followed by many years spent in learning the skills of the trade and its esoteric wisdom. That is how the master drummer, court troubadour or griot is able to play out the history of his people. They are close to the ancestors and the deeper undercurrents of society.

This concern for origins or roots is evident in the 'Awakening', played by the drummers at the start of the Ashanti Adae Festival. Before anything else can begin the drums play homage to the ancestors for providing the drum materials, like cedar wood and elephant skin — as well as to the ancestor of all drummers.

Besides containing the cool and collected wisdom of the ancestors and society as a whole, the local music of Africa sparks off hot, disoriented states where the grip of the dance-beat becomes that of possession by the spiritual archetypes of a particular Beat. So strong is this African idea of dance as body-prayer that it has influenced Christian sects such as the African Separatist Churches, the Soul and Spirituals of America and the Pocomania and Rastafarianism of the Caribbean.

Not only does African music spread wisdom and knowledge, but it is also used to send messages. Not coded ones, but spoken ones played on the tonal drums, by imitating the meaningful tones of Africa's tonal languages. When the first Europeans visited Kumasi, the capital of the Ashanti Empire, they were told that the drums were discussing the current situation of the Napoleonic Wars. The news of a big British defeat in the Ashanti Wars was known in Sierra Leone by the local people, before the British there, because of this 'bush telegraph'.

Traditional dancers

104

African music is not just a tool for social control, it is also an instrument of satire and protest. In the olden days a chief could be literally drummed out of town by the young warrior associations and the secret masked societies. There were even musical duals. Musicians were court jesters and social critics, a tradition that is as still as strong as ever.

African musical traditions accommodate change as each generation brings its own ideas and styles, modifying older ones. Even the traditional or 'cultural' music which abounds in Africa today is not a fossilised remnant, but rather the product of thousands of years of experimenting and honing down.

The balance of sound and silence

What of the music itself which generates its own power from a dynamic balancing of material and non-material, sound and silence, the heat of the rhythms and the cool of the beat? Hot rhythms whose sound energy is produced by the clash and interplay of the cross-rhythms and which in turn create space and time.

Space is left as the rhythms are only linked at critical junctions or intersections. The whole network of rhythmic sounds and spaces is locked together like the steel and air of scaffolding. Thus the space and silences between the sounds, are as important as the sounds themselves — whether they are the void between the threads of cross-rhythms, the gaps that pairs of rhythms leave for one another in their dialogue, or even the

Traditional drummer

awareness of the binary impulses of each individual rhythm — the silent upstroke and played downstroke of the drummers, dancers and clappers. This is why African descendants in the New World were able to turn European rhythm inside out, and created space for Jazz and Reggae.

The criss-crossing rhythms of various lengths finally link up as a complete time-cycle. The Beat pulsates within the time-cycle creating an 'inside rhythm', which extends, shortens and bends the time spans of the individual rhythms — an aural equivalent to the optical illusion of shortening, lengthening and bending lines. The hot rhythms of Africa make space and bend time, releasing an almost infinite permutation of spaces and times.

With such a complicated pattern of interwoven sounds and spaces, how is it possible to play African music at all? To the uninitiated it is a wild 'freak-out'. The trick is to be able to flip at will from focusing on sound to focusing on silence, from figure to background. A similar skill is that of the wood carver, who chips away matter to produce space and inner form, for the shape of the carving exists at the boundary of wood and space. In the same way the African musician gives music an inner stability or shape by cutting holes in sound and being able to hear the silence. Only then can the beat really be appreciated and utilised as an anchoring point within the sea of rhythms. The Beat is not only the totality of the sounds but also of all the silent gaps and spaces. This is the 'hidden rhythm', a stillness within the turmoil of sounds, like the quiet in the eye of a storm.

It's not only what is played that matters, but also what is not sounded — understatement rather than overstatement. This laid-back and cooled-down approach can only be achieved after first mastering all the individual rhythms. Only after many years is it possible to become a master musician, who can balance sound and silence. The master musician knows when to come in to strengthen a flagging rhythm, or create a silence, or jump into the silence and improvise. In other words the master is poised between cool silence and hot sounds, the hidden rhythm and the overt beat.

Ibrahim Abdulai, a Ghanaian drummer, expounds some African musical wisdom:

Mustapha Tetteh Addy, one of Ghana's top master drummers

'We say that music is sweet when it is cool, or "baalim" — not "cool" in the way that water or the weather is cool, but rather it means "slow" or "gentle". The young men play "yirin" or "by heart". They don't cool their bodies and take their time. If you do something that is not necessary, if you are rude or rough, if you miss your road and go to the wrong place, that is yirin, it has no meaning. The young people dance faster and they usually play faster too. When they are playing, before an old man will play this or that, the young man is already on top of it. Sometimes when you know something too much, you can do it in a rough way and add something unnecessary inside. If you beat a drum very hard the sound will reduce. And if your wrist is too fast, your drum will not sound. "My wrist is fast," that is not drumming. As you are beating, it is your heart that is talking, and what your heart is going to say, your hand will collect it and play. Unless you cool your heart, your drumming will not stand.'

(From *African rhythms and African Sensibility* by John Chernoff. Published by Chicago University Press)

The African master musician is not only in tune with the music, but also with the society at large. He leads through balance and co-operation. He can hot people up into states of possession or cool them down by focusing on inner silence. Music is a microcosm of the whole society.

African music is composed of many rhythms or polyrhythms (rather than a single one as in Europe). Likewise Africans are traditionally polytheistic (have many gods and goddesses), polygamous (have several spouses), polyglot (speak more than one language) and they may live in compound houses.

This pluralism and psychic space gives the traditional system of ritual and protocol much flexibility. There is conformity to the rules, taboos and regulations and yet spaces or options are left at certain critical positions. Symbolic periods of freedom and chaos, upside-down behaviour and ritual licence that punctuate individual and social life.

Poise is therefore a prime virtue needed in balancing these cycles of freedom and necessity, chaos and order, a virtue that comes only with maturity. Hence the great respect for age in Africa, whether for the master musician, elder or ancestor. Mature wisdom is ultimately obtained by an awareness of the silence and stillness enmeshed within the bustle and noise of everyday life. This gives the African sage stability. Black Americans call it 'Daddy Cool'.

Music is a microcosm of society and African music embodies all the unspoken traditional wisdom of that continent. Black music and Black art are bringing this ancient African wisdom to the modern world — the art of expressing space and time symbolically, and participating in that expression through the moving body.

2 First Fusions – Orchestras and Brass Bands

Traditional African music is flexible and ever-changing from generation to generation. There have been cross-overs and feed back, Western influences on African music and African influences on Western music.

Modernised traditional music and dance styles that developed along the West African coast in the nineteenth century, demonstrate the subtlety of the interaction between Black and White music – styles such as Gome Ashiko, Timo and Osibisaaba; rhythms that later were incorporated into Highlife and Juju music.

Even though no European instruments were used in these first fusions, the songs were sung in hymn-type harmonies. European carpentry techniques were used for construction – new brands of African drums, such as the square tambourines and the giant Gome drum. Gome, Gombe or Goumbeh music was popular not only in West Africa but also in the Caribbean. Another type of drum that was much simpler to make than the local hand-carved drums, was the barrel drum, made by coopers with planks and iron hoops.

While some African musicians started to incorporate new ideas into their music, others began playing in Brass Bands, regimental bands and dance orchestras.

In the poorer areas of port towns, local musicians learnt to play sailors' instruments and created a blend that became known as Palm-Wine music, Ragtimes or 'Native Blues'. This developed into guitar band music, brass bands and orchestras.

The brass bands go all the way back to military brass and fyfe bands associated with the coastal forts. European, West Indian and African musicians were employed to work at these forts. They played military Marches, Polkas, Waltzes and fusions of their own.

Konkomba music

About a hundred years ago, a type of African brass band music called Adaha became very popular with the many brass bands in the Fanti areas of Ghana. Within a short time the whole of the South of Ghana was swinging to this music, and every town of note wanted to have its own brass band.

When local musicians couldn't afford to buy the expensive imported instruments they made do with drums, voices, and plenty of fancy dress. This poor man's brass band music, with its drill-like dances, became known as 'Konkomba' music; taking its name from the exotic gear of the Konkomba people of northern Ghana.

Beni and dance orchestras

A similar thing happened in East Africa when, around the turn of the century, military brass band music was taken up by local people. They combined African and European drums, bugles and brass instruments with military parade type dances – and called it 'Beni'. This Beni Ngoma, or Beni dance craze, was spread around the rural hinterland of East Africa by the Askaris or local African troops during the First World War period. It became progressively Africanised. For instance, the trumpet was replaced by the gourd, Kazoo. This led to a whole number of even more Africanised dance styles like the Magonda, Kalela and Chikosa.

Another popular type of music at around the turn of the century was performed by the African dance orchestras, complete with brass, woodwind and stringed instruments. The Black and mulatto élites in the towns, especially liked them. There were orchestras such as the Lagos City Orchestra in Nigeria, the Excelsior Orchestra in Accra, the Don't Worry Entertainers of South Africa, and the Dapa Dan Jazz Band of Sierra Leone.

These large and prestigious orchestras played waltzes, foxtrots, quicksteps, ragtimes and other ballroom dance numbers for their top-hatted audiences. Then, they began to orchestrate the local melodies and street music. That's how Highlife got its name.

These 'stylish' orchestras went on playing right up to the Second World War times and then died out. During this war, tens of thousands of Allied troops were stationed in Africa, and African soldiers fought in Burma and elsewhere. All this affected the popular music scene in Africa. Jazz and Swing became all the rage.

So the huge orchestras gave way to the smaller Jazz combo of the post-war period. The man who pioneered this breakthrough was E.T. Mensah.

3 E.T. Mensah, the King of Highlife

E.T. Mensah, or E.T. as he is known, was born in Accra in 1919, and became known as the King of Highlife. It was his band, the Tempos, which pioneered urban Highlife, played by dance bands. E.T. started his musical career when, as a small boy, he joined the Accra Orchestra as a flute player. The Accra Orchestra was formed by Teacher Lamptey around 1930, based on his schoolboy band.

Teacher Lamptey, the headmaster of a James Town elementary school, had been a member of one of the first dance orchestras in Ghana, the Jazz Kings, formed in the early twenties. But it was his Accra Orchestra that became the most well-known pre-war orchestra, and many of Ghana's top musicians passed through it, such as E.T., Joe Kelly and Tommy Gripman.

E.T. and his older brother Yebuah then went on to form their own Accra Rhythmic Orchestra which won the Lambeth Walk Dance Competition in 1939 at the King George Memorial Hall (now Parliament House).

Yebuah Mensah comments on the origin of the term 'highlife':

During the early twenties, during my childhood, the term "Highlife" was created by people who gathered around the dancing clubs such as the Rodger Club (built in 1904) to watch and listen to the couples enjoying themselves. Highlife started as a catch-name for the indigenous songs played at these clubs by such early bands as the Jazz Kings, the Cape Coast Sugar

E.T. and J. Mallet, members of the Accra Rhythmic Orchestra in 1937

Babies, the Sekondi Nanshamang and later the Accra Orchestra. The people outside called it "Highlife" as they did not reach the class of the couples going inside, who not only had to pay a, then, relatively high entrance fee of 7s. 6d., but also had to wear full evening dress including top-hats.

E.T. Mensah was self-taught at first:

He taught himself music, starting with the flute. During World War Two, saxophonist Sgt. Leopard of the British Army in West Africa, looking for musicians, took him under his tutelage. From him, E.T. learnt how to play the alto saxophone. He took to playing the trumpet and

later led the Accra Tempos Band. E.T. claims that it was watching and listening to Eddie Calvert play Cherry Pink and Apple Blossom that encouraged him to play the trumpet the way he does now. Many musicians in Ghana have passed through his hands; many more extending outside Ghana have modelled their style on his. His music was recorded by Decca (West Africa) and admirers gave him the title "King of Highlife".

(*Mensah's African Rhythms:*
Record Notes)

The high-class dance orchestras were eclipsed during the Second World War, when American and British troops were stationed in Ghana. They brought in Jazz and Swing. Night-clubs and dives were opened for them with names like Kalamazoo, Weekend-in-Havanna and the New York Bar. They also set up dance combos and played with local musicians.

Jazz and swing

The first combo was the Black and White Spots, set up by Sergeant Leopard. E.T. Mensah left his brother's orchestra and joined up with Leopard's Jazz combo as sax player, in 1940. Sergeant Leopard, a Scot, had been a professional saxophonist in England and according to E.T. it was Leopard himself who taught them Jazz techniques:

It was Sergeant Leopard who taught us the correct

methods of intonation, vibrato, tongueing and breath control, which contributed to place us above the average standard in the town. **"**

Just after the war, E.T. went on to join the Tempos, set up by the Ghanaian pianist Adolf Doku and an English engineer Arthur Harriman. At first the band included some White soldiers but after the war, when the Europeans left, the band became completely African and E.T. became its leader. It was a seven-piece band with E.T. doubling on trumpet and sax, Joe Kelly on tenor sax and Guy Warren on drums.

Guy Warren made an important contribution as he had been playing Afro-Cuban music and calypsos in England. So the Tempos not only played with a Jazz touch, but incorporated Calypsos into their repertoires and added the bongos and maraccas to the line-up.

It was the Tempos' style of Highlife that became all the rage; so that by the early fifties the band started touring West Africa, and recording for Decca. E.T., who had been a pharmacist, was able to go fully professional.

It was during the fifties that E.T. was acclaimed the King of Highlife throughout West Africa, for although the palm-wine variety of Highlife was popular in the rural areas of West Africa, ballroom music and colonial-type orchestras still dominated the urban dance scene.

For instance, in Nigeria, Highlife music like Konkomba, Juju and Palm-Wine music was left to the rural and low-class urban night-spots. High-class clubs featured dance bands like Bobby Benson's, Sammy Akpabot's and the Empire Hotel Band, which played only Swing and Ballroom music. But E.T.'s style of Highlife soon began to influence them and create a whole new generation of Nigerian dance band musicians like Victor Olaiya, Eddie Okunta, Arinze and Rex Lawson, Charles Iwegbue, Victor Chukwu, Chief Billy Friday, Enyang Henshaw, King Kennytone and Roy Chicago.

The Tempos affected not only these mature Nigerian dance band musicians, but also the young Victor Uwaifo whose guitar band was to become so popular later on. As Dan Acquaye, one of E.T.'s musicians, recalls from one of the many Tempos tours of Nigeria:

" In Benin City, Victor Uwaifo, then a schoolboy, would rush down to our hotel after school to watch my cousin Dizzy Acquaye on the guitar. He was determined to play the guitar and used to help Dizzy clean his instrument. **"**

Victor Uwaifo corroborates his story:

" I used to see E.T. Mensah and his Tempos play whenever they they were in Benin and I went to see their guitarist Dizzy Acquaye to put me through a few chords. I had a guitar book but I didn't understand the chord drawings. Dizzy helped me. **"**

Many musicians went on to form their own bands, modelled on the Tempos — Joe Kelly, Tommy Gripman, Saka Acquaye, Spike Anyankor, Ray Ellis, and the first female vocalist Juliana Okine — all from Ghana; and Zeal Onyia and Babyface Paul Osamade from Nigeria.

E.T. on tour

During the fifties, the Tempos toured West African countries, where there were no Highlife dance bands. In Sierra Leone there was local Palm-Wine music and Meringue, but this was never

The Tempos dance band in the mid-fifties

played by the dance bands there. So E.T.'s music was an instant success. They played at a party for the Prime Minister, Doctor Margai, and toured the country. By the early sixties, dance bands there, like the Ticklers, were in full swing, playing both Highlifes and Meringues.

In Liberia, too, local music was not being played by the dance bands. They were playing the Quadrille, a refined Creole music that the American Liberian freed slaves brought over from the Southern states of America. In fact the Tempos were so popular in Liberia that President Tubman invited them over for his inauguration. He sent them the following telegram.

❛ I am very pleased to note that you and your band have safely arrived in Accra. We enjoyed the melody, rhythm and tempo of your band and this telegram constitutes an invitation to you and your band to return for the inauguration. ❜

In the French-speaking countries of Guinea and Ivory Coast, E.T. did not even come across an African dance band or orchestra, let alone one playing indigenous music. In the night-clubs of Conakry and Abidjan he heard White groups playing French music. The Tempos even had to show the people there how to dance Highlife.

E.T. Mensah's Tempos spread Highlife far and wide, until E.T. retired in the 1970s.

The late Bobby Benson's band

4 Palm-Wine and Guitars

In spite of their prestigious beginnings, the large dance bands and brass bands have all but died out, and almost everywhere in Africa it is the up-dated Palm-Wine music that dominates the local music scene. This is in spite of the fact that Palm-Wine music emerged from low-class seaport dives and Palm-Wine bars. In fact the guitar became so closely associated with this African beer, brewed naturally from the palm-tree, that anyone playing the guitar was considered to be a drunken rascal.

Where sea shanties met African music, Palm-Wine music was born. The line-up was a combination of local African instruments and those of the sailors — the guitar, concertina, accordion, harmonica and banjo. Compared to the classy orchestral instruments, these instruments were cheap and portable.

But it was the guitar that became the main melody instrument. It was probably introduced to Africa by Portuguese sailors, thus completing yet another circuit in the complex to and fro of contemporary African music; for the Spanish guitar has its roots in Muslim North Africa from where it was taken to Spain and Portugal in medieval times.

The first Africans to make the modern guitar their own, were the Kru or Kroo fishermen who lived in villages along the coast of Liberia. When the Europeans came, the Kroos became famous as seamen on the old sailing and steam ships. They also became famous for their guitar playing, and their African styles like 'Dagomba', 'Fireman' and 'Mainline' accompanied them wherever they went. 'Dagomba' was an 'exotic' name they gave to one of their new styles, naming it after a tribe that lived in the interior; 'Fireman' probably got its name from the coal-burning steamships. 'Mainline' is the first and fundamental style taught when learning African finger-picking guitar styles.

These styles, and others that grew out of them, spread right through West and Central Africa, ending up in East and Southern Africa by the 1950s.

Palm-Wine music was introduced to Sierra Leone in the twenties by Kroos living in Freetown's Kroo-town quarter where it was known as 'Ragtime'. Kroos, such as Foster and the seaman Eku, played their guitars in the red light district of Freetown, accompanied by the giant bass 'hand-piano', called the Congoma. Other groups featured the guitar and African percussion with the musical saw. Examples of these groups are Peter na Leopard and Waking Profit who acquired most of their money from wake-keepings. Most popular of all was Ebeneezer Calendar who raised the status of Palm-Wine music, and whose guitar band used the sousaphone to provide the bass line. His Meringues, Calypsos and Highlifes were popular right up to the sixties.

It was Ghanaian Palm-Wine music, which started at the same time as that of Sierra Leone, that made the first major shift from the coast to the interior and hinterland. This happened when the Akans went guitar mad and added 'Ashanti Blues' to the palm-wine repertoire. This is basically their own local music in which the traditional lute or seprewah was replaced by the guitar.

By the thirties and forties there were dozens of guitar bands from various Akan areas — Kwerku Bibi, Kwese Manu, Kwese Peperah, Mireku, Yaw Ofori and Appiah Adjekum. This list is endless, but the first of all was Kwame Asare or 'Sam' as he is fondly remembered in Ghana.

In Ghana, during the early fifties, Palm-Wine music was linked up with acting. Before this, the concert parties and comic trios had been accompanied by ballroom music. It was E.K. Nyame from Ghana who made the vital connection between Highlife and Concert Parties. His music became an inspiration throughout Africa during the fifties. By the end of the fifties the guitar bands started going electric.

The birth of Juju

Palm-Wine music appeared in western Nigeria in the thirties where it became known as Juju music. This was, in fact, a combination of traditional Yoruba music with modernised African styles, like Gome or Gombe (found all over West Africa), Ashiko (an early name for highlife) and Konkomba (which spread out from Ghana). Juju music also incorporated contemporary Yoruba street music like Denge, played on guitar and samba drum and Ayidigbo, played on 'hand-piano' and drums.

The actual name 'Juju' was coined by a mandolin player called the Tunde King in the late 1930s. Other formative Juju musicians were Ojoge Daniels who played ukelele and banjo, the guitarist Ayinde Bakare and the Ayidigbo player Adeolu Akinsanyu, who later formed the Rio Lindo Orchestra. Then, in the fifties, I.K. Dairo turned Juju electric.

In central and eastern Nigeria Palm-Wine music, known there as 'Native Blues', first surfaced in the thirties with Igbo guitarists like Israel Nwaba and G.T. Owuka. In the early fifties N.K. Nyame's music became immensely popular in eastern Nigeria and guitar bands there were influenced by his Akan Trio — like those of Aderi Olariechi from Owerri, January from Port Harcourt and Okonkwo Adigwe from Asaba.

Similar to the Palm-Wine music of West Africa was Dansi music from East Africa, the coastal music of freed slaves. They used sailors' instruments to play local and imported melodies. Unlike its West African counterpart however, Dansi went 'stylish' by incorporating orchestral instruments and so suffered the same fate as the West African dance orchestras — it died out!

The palm-wine music that originated from the Kroos of West Africa did finally reach East Africa in the fifties. It was introduced from Zaire where, in the forties, people had gone crazy over the West African finger picking style of guitar playing. In 1952 Jean Bosco (Mwenda Wa Bayeke) began to release Rumbas and local Luba music played on Spanish guitar. This style is quite different from the distinctive 'Congo-jazz' style of electric guitar playing that grew out of it in the sixties. Another early finger-style top guitarist from Zaire was Losta Abelo whose music, like that of Bosco, spread into East Africa during the fifties. It influenced musicians, there like John Mwale, Paul Muchupa and Fundi Koude. Later everything went electric.

However, non-electric guitar music remains popular in East Africa is evident in the success of Daniel Kachamba of Kenya who entertains everyone by singing songs while playing guitar, harmonica, bass-drum and rattle at the same time.

5 'Sam', The First Palm-Wine Guitarist

The man who spread the palm-wine style far afield was the Ghanaian guitarist Kwame Asare or 'Sam' as he is usually known. He combined the various African seamen's styles like Dagomba, Fireman and Mainline, with the more indigenous and rural 'Native Blues' (this is a minor chord music played in 3/4 time rather than 4/4 and usually sung in the vernacular).

It was Sam who composed the famous Highlife standard *Yaa Amponsah*, a song about a beautiful and alluring 'good-time girl', and a song which laid down the basis for hundreds of others. In many ways *Yaa Amponsah* is to Highlife what the twelve-bar blues is to Jazz.

Sam and his Trio went to England in the mid-twenties, and recorded and released scores of their Palm-Wine Highlifes on the Zonophone label (EZ Series).

Sam's nephew is another famous Ghanaian palm-wine guitarist, Kwaa Mensah. Although Sam died in the 1950s, Kwaa is still playing his uncle's style of music right up to today. Kwaa comments on his Uncle Sam's early life:

Sam was born in 1903 in Cape Coast. His father played the concertina and used to take Sam, when he was very small, on his shoulder to play clips. His father played Adaha, the music of the flute, fife and brass bands. And also Opim and Ohuga (native blues). Opim was a special rhythm for the concertina. Another rhythm they played was Ashiko, a highlife played with concertina or accordian, clips and carpenter's saw, where the saw is bent and an iron is used to rattle its face. Sam later learnt to play guitar, against the wishes of his father, who thought only ruffians played guitar. So Sam ran away to Kumasi, where he met Kwah Kantah from El Mina and H.E. Biney from Cape Coast. Kwah Kantah played wooden box and Biney and Sam played guitars. In 1928 they went to London to make recordings.

Kwaa Mensah was born in Lagos and brought up in Cape Coast. He describes how he was taught guitar by Sam.

My uncle Sam taught me to play guitar in 1937 and anywhere he goes, I go with him. We were entertaining the soldiers during the war at Cape Coast, Kumasi and Accra. We made music and mime for the soldiers and army officers. I was the singer and clips player and Sam was playing guitar, singing and changing costumes. He used to dress up as a Sierra Leonese woman and sometimes as an Ashanti woman.

Kwaa continues his story:

Before the war I was in an Adaha band called the Antwem band. I didn't use guitar in this band, I played pati (a small side drum) and fifes. In 1939 the Silver Stars Konkomba group was formed and I left the Antwem band. The Konkomba band has jazz drums, pati-drums, bass alto and tenor tambourines and thirty singers. I was the first to bring guitar to them. We played Adaha: Adesim, which is a fast Highlife; Ashanti (Native) Blues; Rumbas; Foxtrots; Bumps-a-daisy; Sambas; La congas; Spanish music and Dagomba Highlifes. I went on to form my own Akote Special Konkomba group and left when the war finished. When the war finished, Konkomba finished. By this time I was a master guitarist and formed the Navy Blues, which used giant bass hand-piano, pati, tambourines, cigarette tin and clips. The Navy Blues band collapsed when I went to Kumasi in 1951, and when I came back I formed Kwaa Mensah's Band, which had the same instruments. My first recordings were with His Masters Voice (HMV now part of EMI) and we were paid £5 for each side (i.e. £10 a record). Altogether I made nearly 200 records for them.

Although Kwaa is over 60 years old he is still active in the music business. He is still playing and is an Inspector of the Musicians' Union of Ghana (MUSIGA), empowered to check pirating.

6 E.K. Nyame's Music and Drama

E.K. Nyame was born in 1927 in Ghana. He revolutionised West African music in the 1950s, as he not only updated the Highlife music of the Palm-Wine groups, but also combined it with the acting of the local concert groups.

Like Highlife music, the Ghanaian concert parties or comic opera groups, started off, around the turn of the century, as stylish affairs in the towns. Again, like Highlife, they rapidly spread into the rural hinterland where they were indigenised. When Highlife bands left the towns with their orchestras, the music was known as Palm-Wine music and was played by guitar bands. When concert parties like the Axim Trio and Jovial Jokers moved into the villages, they incorporated Ananse, the traditional spider-hero, in their acts. Their Joker or 'Bob' took on all the mischevious aspects of Ananse.

However, the music of the early concert parties remained basically Western Ballroom music: Fox-trots, Quicksteps and Rag-times, played on harmonium and jazz-drums.

E.K. Nyame completed this process of Africanisation of the concert party, by using Highlife guitar bands for the music. He also started using the local language in the plays instead of English. His combination of Highlife and concert acting was an instant success. From 1951, when he formed the Akan Trio, practically all the guitar bands in Ghana linked up with acting groups. In the fifties E.K.'s band was the supreme guitar band. He became Nkrumah's favourite musician and accompanied him on many state visits. Also many of E.K.'s songs and plays supported Nkrumah and the Independence movement. During the fifties E.K. recorded over four hundred records for Decca, Queen-aphone and HMV and he became popular throughout Black Africa.

I was fortunate to know him, and often visited him at his house in James Town, Accra where he gave me some tips on guitar-playing and let me interview him. E.K. joined his first group, Appiah Adjekum's band in 1948, when he was just a clerk:

It was an amateur group and if anyone wanted to make some outdooring (christening) or function we would go there. I played the rhythm guitar and Adjekum played the Hawaiian guitar. There were three oblong tambourines covered in velum. The bass one was sat on (a Gome drum). We also had a four-corner (con-certina) and castanets or claves. Adjekum's wife played the guitar.

E.K. explained why he left this band:

I had the idea of modernising the music to raise the stan-dard. At first we used tambour-ines, guitar and clips, but we made a change in 1951 and replaced the tambourines with bongos, jazz-drums and fiddle bass.

What of the Akan Trio's early days?

We staged in English but there were parts of it when a character came in and spoke our dialect (Twi). But we minded the colonial ideology and British mind, so whatever we did in those days was in English. But by 1957 we were using Twi. We were the first concert to use guitar band, and the first to use Spanish bongos. We played Highlifes, Ragtimes, and Calypsos on rare occasions. I played the Gentleman and Bob. We introduced the show with an opening chorus, a quickstep sung in English.

E.K. described how he got ideas for his stories:

When we created a very good Highlife number, it's out of this we built our concert story. Because the whole nation wants to see us performing what we have done on the recording side. One play was called "When you push plantain you have to push banana" (i.e. you have to treat everyone equally). It was about a man who married two wives but loved one more than the other, and the son of the one he rejected became a chief somewhere else. Later on the father became poor and wretched. And it was the child he neglected that came to his aid and who came and brought the father up again.

E.K. died in 1977. His body was laid out on a golden bed and he was given a state funeral attended by ten thousand people.

Section Five
Music Business

Musicians' Union march through
Accra, Ghana in 1979

1 The African Recording Industry

Early days

Believe it or not, the African record business goes all the way back to 1907, when records were first sold in South Africa — at two shillings each! The main companies were the French-owned Pathe and British-owned Zonophone. By 1914, 100,000 records a year were being sold there.

In the twenties, other foreign companies came onto the scene. His Master's Voice (HMV), for instance, sold over one million records in South Africa in 1927; and started recording 'native' songs, as did Zonophone and Brunswick at about the same time.

During the thirties, Black South African close-harmony and rag-time groups modelled on Afro-American groups became very popular. Many of them were sent to England to record, for instance, with EMI (formed by the merger of HMV, Zonophone and Columbia in 1931).

In the forties, the first African record company was set up. This was Gallo-Africa, which employed the first African talent scouts and producers like Griffiths Motsieloa. Their initial major success was August Musurugwa's hit song *Skokian*, which he sold for a few pounds, and which made Gallo-Africa hundreds of thousands of pounds.

In East Africa, records in English and Hindi were first imported in the early twenties. But by the late twenties HMV, Odeon, Columbia, Zonophone and Pathe were recording and releasing local African music, sung in Swahili,

Luganda and Somali. For instance, in 1939 HMV/Zonophone sold over 200,000 records, of which 80,000 were in the vernacular languages of East Africa.

West Africa lagged a bit behind, but by 1930, when HMV/Zonophone released 180,000 records there, they had come level. During the period 1930 to 1933 the major record companies sold 8,000,000 records in West Africa.

During the Second World War, record production remained low because of the war effort. Afterwards it started up again and during the fifties, records of African and European artists were flooding into Africa. Columbia, for instance, released over 2,000 different records of African artists in its East Africa Series. In 1954 they even had a major hit with an African song in Britain. They made a quarter of a million pounds from South African Aaron Lerole's penny-whistle tune *Tom Harke*.

Decca launched its West Africa Series in 1947, when almost 50,000 records were released of top Ghanaian, Nigerian and Sierra Leonese artists. So successful was this that a permanent studio was built near Accra and portable equipment sent to Lagos twice a year. By the end of the fifties, Decca West Africa was pressing almost a quarter of a million singles a year.

The biggest recording company in Africa operating from France during the fifties, was Pathe-Marconi, which had offices in Nigeria, Kenya and South Africa.

The first pressing plants actually built in Africa were those of Gallo-Africa, EMI and Pathe-Marconi in South Africa, all fully operational in the fifties. Then in the early sixties Phonogram (Polygram) and EMI built pressing plants in Nigeria.

The situation today – South Africa

Today in South Africa records are still mostly produced by the big companies, like home-grown Gallo-Africa and the foreign multi-nationals Pathe-Marconi and EMI. But many, especially the singles, are being made by the many small local companies, such as Imbongi, HVN, Soweto, Shonalanga and Smanjo Manje. These companies deal exclusively in singles of popular songs — Jives, Kwela music, traditional songs and Township music. They are usually sung in Zulu, Shona and Sotho.

The problems facing the South African local music industry are many. But surprisingly, in spite of the undemocratic political system, there are effective copyright laws, a problem that still has not been solved in the rest of Black Africa. In 1964 the South African government introduced record royalties, and the record companies agreed to pay them, as there is great competition for popular Black artists, who often sell gold discs on the local market.

But there is still opposition to the idea of copyrighting African music from those who argue that

African music is communal and modern tunes are re-workings of traditional ones. This seemingly 'democratic' idea has become, in the hands of some producers, simply another way of ripping-off Black artists. Particularly so in the case of certain White producers of exotic 'African tribal musicals', who do not want to pay royalties for the African dances and compositions they use.

In spite of the copyright laws, the number of Black musicians who register and claim royalties are few and far between. Many are illiterate and are in the hands of paternalistic companies who organise their savings right up to retirement. These companies prefer to have salaried musicians whom they can move about at will, rather than complete bands. In this way it becomes difficult to pinpoint copyright and the company producers can therefore claim it.

As if these problems were not enough, the apartheid political system has two direct negative effects on the Black music business. Firstly the musicians are not allowed to form their own trade union and therefore they remain as a pool of unorganised and easily exploitable labour. Secondly many of South Africa's top Black artists, who sing out against their racialist government, have had to flee abroad.

Today – East Africa

The big multi-nationals in East Africa are Phonogram (Polygram), EMI, Pathe-Marconi and Decca. The first local East Africa company was the Jambo label, begun in Kenya just after the Second World War. Today there are dozens of small local record companies printing singles of popular guitar band music, hymns and Afro-Swahili Tarab music, companies like AIT in Kenya and the Seychelles, ACPI in Kenya, Ray's Music Room in the Seychelles, the Green Carpet in Zambia, Discomad in Madagascar and the Tanzanian Film company which produces half a million singles a year in Tanzania.

In East Africa, very few albums are pressed and the market is mainly in singles. It is a very small market, with a top single selling around fifty thousand copies. According to Hans Kinzl, who was Managing Director of Phonogram East Africa, 'the market is so small that in one year we only sell as many records in East Africa as we do one good record in Europe or the States'. The album market is so tiny, that when EMI set up its pressing plant in Nairobi in 1976, it kept going by manufacturing 100,000 records a year for the Nigerian market.

Pirating is another problem in the music business, and pirate cassette production has almost become a cottage industry in East Africa, one which has cut deeply into the profits of record companies there, both foreign and local. It has become so bad that the Kenyan government has tried to outlaw pirating.

Another problem in Kenya was the introduction in 1978 of a fifty-five per cent sales tax on records. Ron Andrews, who runs AIT, reckons it has become cheaper to import records than to manufacture the records locally.

1978 was also a bad year for EMI in Nairobi, for that was the year the Nigerian government banned the import of records. EMI therefore lost its Nigerian market and the factory had to close down.

Generally speaking the East African record business is far smaller than that of West Africa and is lagging behind.

Today – West Africa

The main international companies catering for the huge local market in Zaire and the French-speaking West African countries are Decca, Phonogram (Polygram) and WEA Fillipachi, a subsidiary of Warner Brothers. Decca has just brought out an eighty-page catalogue of its African records and cassettes. WEA Fillipachi has just set up an office in the Ivory Coast and organised a thirty-two day African concert tour (Africa Special) of its artists.

French-based companies in West Africa are Pathe-Marconi, now in decline; Safari Ambiance which releases albums of artists from Zaire, the Cameroons, Ivory Coast, Upper Volta and Gabon; and Sono-Disc which releases records and cassettes of artists from the Ivory Coast, the Cameroons and Zaire.

The record business of the French-speaking West African countries is generally behind that of the English-speaking ones. Most of the production has been in the hands of the international companies, especially those based in France. For instance at the 13th International Trade Fair of Record and Musical Productions (MIDEM) held at Cannes in 1979, only three African record producers attended, from Nigeria,

Algeria and South Africa. There were none from the French-speaking African countries. However, things are beginning to change. Local recording studios and pressing plants are now being set up in Zaire, Ivory Coast and Senegal. In Togo there is the 24 track Studio de la Nouvelle Marche and in the Republic of Benin a 24 track studio is about to be set up by Bernard Dohounzo of SATEL.

In the English-speaking countries of West Africa like Sierra Leone, Liberia, Ghana and Nigeria, the local record industry is more developed, especially in Ghana and Nigeria where albums are now more important than singles.

In Ghana there are four recording studios: the eight-track Ghanaian Ambassador Studio near Kumasi; the Ghana Film studio in Accra which has just gone over from 2 track to 8 track; a recently opened 8 track studio at Faisal Helwani's Napoleon Club; and the 4 track Polygram studio, also in Accra (now closed).

There are two pressing plants in the country: Ambassador Records which presses as well as records, and the Record Manufacturers of Ghana Limited which is fifty per cent owned by Polygram. Between 1969 and 1975 Polygram was producing half a million singles and a hundred thousand albums a year. But by the mid-seventies the whole of the Ghanaian record business met with many difficulties, due to the general economic decline of the country. Record production went down to one quarter of its former total. This created a bottleneck in the industry which had several serious repercussions. Many of Ghana's top musicians and bands went abroad to record and often never returned home, like Eddie Quansah, Bob Pinado, Boombaya, Pat Thomas, Oscar Sulley, Kiki Gyan, Kofi Ayivor, Basa-Basa and Jeff Tagoe. As local music could not be produced the music market was flooded with funk and disco music.

March against the Government

By the late seventies things got so bad that the Musicians' Union (MUSIGA) organised a march on the seat of government at the Castle in Accra. The government finally woke up to the situation. They broke the monopoly of the two pressing companies and redistributed record vinyl to independent producers. They reduced the retail price of records dramatically and ordered that seventy-five per cent of all vinyl imported into the country should be used to manufacture local music, rather than imported music under licence. The Prices and Incomes Board collected over one hundred thousand pounds in unpaid record royalties and passed it on to musicians who were owed money.

Whereas Ghana has been suffering from serious economic problems, Nigeria was enjoying an oil boom, which boosted the record industry (records are actually made from oil). The record business was also helped in 1978, when the government banned the import of records. By 1979 Nigeria was pressing all its own records, which that year numbered twelve million albums (twenty million in 1982).

Today there are many pressing plants in the country. The largest is the Record Manufacturers of Nigeria Limited at Ikeja, which can press up to twenty thousand albums a day. RMNL is jointly owned by Decca (35%), EMI (25%), Take Your Choice Records (20%) and Northern Nigerian Investment Limited (20%).

Polygram has a large pressing plant in Lagos. It is sixty per cent Nigerian-owned and can manufacture four million records a year. Then there is the record factory of the Apala King, Haruna Ishola. This was opened in 1979 near Ibadan and is now producing almost a third of Nigerian records. It has a maximum capacity of thirty thousand records a day. There is also a fully automated plant at Onitsha, set up by Prince Tabansi.

Multi-track studios abound in Nigeria these days. One of the first was the ARC 16 track studio, set up in Lagos with the help of the English drummer Ginger Baker. Then came EMI's studio at Apapa. Haruna Ishola has a 24 track studio near Ibadan — facilities that have been used by Sunny Ade, Fela, Tee Mac and Chris Okotie. Prince Tabansi also has a 24 track studio in Onitsha. And Decca's 16 track studio in Lagos is about to go 24. Artists on the Decca label include Ebeneezer Obey, the Oriental Brothers, the Ikengas, Kabaka International, Christie Essien and Manu Dibango.

In fact Nigeria's record industry is so far in advance of that of other African countries, that it is the first country in Black Africa to have its own pop magazine, *Africa Music*, and its Top Ten of best-selling records.

2 African Music Unions

There are no musicians' unions in South or East Africa, but in the West African countries of Ghana and Nigeria, there have been a series of unions since the 1950s.

The first was the Association of Gold Coast Musicians set up in Ghana in the mid-fifties. This was shortlived and was followed in 1961 by the formation of the Ghana Musicians' Union. At this time, the socialist government of Doctor Nkrumah was encouraging unionisation. Government Ministers were actually involved in the launching of the Musicians' Union. They were Techie-Menson and E.K. Dadson. E.K. Dadson had been the lady impersonator and singer for the famous Axim Trio concert party in the thirties, before going into politics, and later into business.

E.T. Mensah became the union's first Chairman, and the executive included top musical personalities like King Bruce of the Black Beats, Kofi Ghanaba (Guy Warren), Joe Kelly, Tommy Gripman and Phillip Gbeho, who composed Ghana's national anthem.

This union, which catered for the dance bands, was able to make significant headway. It forced Decca to double its royalties on each six shilling record from two pence to four pence. Foreign artists were taxed; for instance, Louis Armstrong had to pay the union on his second trip to Ghana in 1962. At its height, the union membership was around two thousand and it became affiliated to the Ghana Trade Union Congress.

The concert parties and guitar bands also set up a union. This was the National Entertainment Association, set up in 1961 by a popular magician called Kobina Segoe and twenty-eight founding concert bands.

Unfortunately both unions were dissolved after the anti-Nkrumah coup of 1966, as they had links with Nkrumah's Convention People's Party. There was even a ban on the movement of concert bands for a time. There were no music unions in Ghana again, until the Musicians' Union of Ghana (MUSIGA) was set up in 1974 by Faisal Helwani, Jerry Hanson of the Ramblers dance band, Stan Plange of the Uhuru band, Don Quarcoo, King Bruce and Sammy Odoh of the Black Beats and E.T. Mensah of the Tempos. Then, a couple of years later, the concert parties and guitar bands organised themselves into the Ghana Co-operative Indigenous Musicians' Society (GHACIMS). The executive included top band leaders like E.K. Nyame, Doctor Gyasi, Kwaa Mensah, Nana Ampadu, Onyina and Love Nortey.

In Nigeria the Musicians' Union (NUM) was formed in 1958 with Bobby Benson as its first President. The union was affiliated to the Nigerian Trade Union Congress. After a year Bobby Benson left to form another rival union with Victor Olaiya, so Chris Ajilo of the Afro-Cubanos band became president; the famous trumpeter Zeal Onyia, vice-president; Stan Plange, treasurer; and Amaefule Ikoro, secretary. One of the first things the NUM did was to organise a demonstration, as Stan Plange explains:

‘It was in 1960 when the preparations for Nigeria's Independence were going on. The Nigerian government was intending to invite Edmundo Ros to come down and play at the National Independence Dance, as Princess Margaret was coming and we understood she liked Edmundo Ros. Victor Olaiya's band was to play second band. So the Nigerian Musicians' Union organised a demonstration to protest against the bringing of a foreign group. About eight or nine hundred of us marched with placards from the Empire Hotel, Idioro, to Government House to petition the Prime Minister Tafawa Balewa. Myself, Zeal, Chris and Amaefule went inside and told him that the contract should be given to the union, who would then form a mass band and select musicians to form a national orchestra for the Independence Dance. He agreed and gave the contract to the union.’

Stan Plange left Nigeria in 1961, Zeal Onyia left for Germany in 1964 and by the mid-sixties the NUM was defunct. But by this time the drummer Bayo Martins had set up another union called the Musicians' Foundation. Stan Plange's comment on this problem of schisms is:

‘You know, there's always been a split in the Nigerian Musicians' Union and I can't remember when there was one united union for as long as six months.’

These splits persisted right through to the seventies, with Victor Olaiya and I.K. Dairo of the Association of Nigerian Musicians on one side, and Bayo Martins, Bobby Benson and Fela Aníkúlápo-Kuti of the Musicians' Foundation on the other, as *Gong*, the Lagos music paper, of November 1974 notes:

> Nigerian musicians are at war with themselves. The two major bodies are at daggers drawn, each accusing the other of vices ranging from imposition and misrepresentation, to lack of organisation and ignorance.

In fact the Nigerian Musicians' Union is today divided into four factions and the Music Foundation is defunct since Bayo Martins has left the country for Germany. Just recently, though, a new constellation of artists has organised the Performing Artists Association of Nigeria (PMAN) patronised by many of Nigeria's top musicians like Sunny Ade, Ebeneezer Obey, Sonny Okosun, Christie Essiens, Niko Mbarga, Victor Uwaifo, Bobby Benson and Laolu Akins — to name just a few. PMAN was formed in 1981 and outdoored at Sunny Ade's Ariya Club. The main aim of this organisation is to put an end to pirating which controls 60% of the Nigerian market. In fact there has been so little control that pirate companies have openly given their names and addresses on the cassettes they copy — with musicians losing out all round. PMAN had obtained official recognition and is gaining wide support and, according to the

Interim executive of MUSIGA in 1979

Variety Entertainment magazine of Nigeria (October 1982), even the Chairman of the Association of Nigerian Musicians, Eddie Okonta, has joined PMAN, claiming that the old Association is dead.

In Ghana the recent economic decline in the music industry has forced musicians to come together which in turn has strengthened the Musicians' Union, MUSIGA. Today, the membership is around five thousand and includes not only dance bands, but guitar bands and cultural groups as well. MUSIGA has become the spearhead for Ghana's musicians and was particularly active from 1979.

That year the union elected more dynamic leaders — Faisal Helwani, Eddie Quansah, C.K. Mann, Stan Plange, Tommy Darling and Sammy Odoh. They immediately organised a vigil in Accra, attended by over ten thousand people. The next day nearly one thousand musicians marched through Accra to the seat of government at the Castle. Their demands were for official recognition and a different approach to the music industry by the authorities. The union believes that music is a

moneymaking commodity for the country, and therefore the government should encourage the building of multi-track studios and enforce copyright laws. Then Ghana could produce good quality home-grown material for the international market and obtain precious foreign exchange.

Two weeks after the musicians' march there was a coup in Ghana, led by young army officers. Part of their 'house-cleaning' operation included sorting out some of the musicians' grievances. This acted as a shot in the arm for MUSIGA which is now working closely with the government to promote Ghanaian music at home and abroad.

After the 31st Revolution of 1982, the entertainment industry suffered a set-back. But by February 1983 things had cooled down enough for the musicians to organise their own People's Defence Committee (PDC) which acted as a ginger-group within the Musicians' Union. In February 1983 the Minister of Culture promised government aid for the country's ailing music industry, including a 24 track studio.

Index